**The
Nepal
Trekker's
Handbook**

THE
NEPAL
TREKKER'S
HANDBOOK

Amy R. Kaplan
With Michael Keller

Illustrations by Jimmy Thapa
Photographs by Stephen Trimble

Mustang Publishing
New Haven

Copyright © 1989 by Amy R. Kaplan

All rights reserved, including the right of reproduction in whole or in part in any form. Publishing in the United States of America by Mustang Publishing Company, Inc., P.O. Box 9327, New Haven, CT 06533. Manufactured and printed in the USA.

Distributed to the trade by Kampmann National Book Network, Lanham, MD & New York, NY

Library of Congress Cataloging in Publication Data

Kaplan, Amy R., 1943-
    The Nepal trekker's handbook / Amy R. Kaplan, with Michael Keller; illustrations by Jimmy Thapa; photographs by Stephen Trimble.
    p.   cm.
    ISBN 0-914457-28-4 : $9.95 (alk. paper)
    1. Hiking--Nepal--Guide-books.   2. Nepal--Description and travel--Guide-books.   I. Keller, Michael.   II. Title.
    GV199.44.N46K36   1989
    915.496--dc20   88-62886
                                                               CIP

Printed on acid-free paper.

10   9   8   7   6   5   4   3   2   1

To Pasang Lama,
for sharing his joy

Acknowledgments

Many people encouraged us with pre-trek inquiries and post-trek reminders, sometimes grim, of the need for this type of book. Special thanks must go to Lincoln School for all the wonderful years spent there organizing and educating teachers and children to the reality and enchantment of trekking.

Thanks to Ray Rodney for his expertise, to Dr. David Schlim of the Himalayan Rescue Association for his support, to Michael Yager for his enthusiasm, to Jimmy Thapa for his humorous perspective, to Adam, Moss, and Lynn for their patience, to Ganga for the rooftop *dahl baht* which fueled the whole project, to Francisco Kjolseth, and to Rollin Riggs.

Amy R. Kaplan
Michael Keller

Contents

Introduction

Most of the people trekking in Nepal fall into one of three categories: overland travelers, tourists, and experienced mountaineers. This book is addressed to the first two groups and is the result of a number of trek-related circumstances:

• frequent requests from novice trekkers for simple, direct, and appropriate advice;

• our knowledge that it is possible to have a wonderful, problem-free trekking experience;

• our understanding that information about small things can make a big difference in planning a successful trek;

• our enthusiasm for Nepal and trekking.

Nepal's tourist industry is growing and changing rapidly as the popularity and accessibility of this magical Kingdom increase. This book is designed to supplement the many comprehensive guidebooks available that recommend specific hotels, restaurants, sightseeing excursions, trek routes, etc. Unfortunately, due to the swiftly changing tourist scene in Nepal, guidebooks become out-dated quickly. Therefore, we recommend you contact a reliable travel agency and/or trekking company for the nitty-gritty details. We've listed a few suggestions in a later chapter.

So, our purpose is to give the general information that trekkers require, plus the "insider tips" that will increase your confidence and enjoyment during a trekking holiday. We list prices when necessary, but please don't take them as gospel, because the Nepalese rupee is frequently devalued relative to the U.S. dollar. Inflation is also a problem, and while you shouldn't worry about financial chaos when you're in Nepal, the economic climate affects both the business of trekking and our ability to give you accurate price information. Please bear this in mind as you plan your trip with this book.

How to Use This Book

We're assuming that you're planning a trek in Nepal and that you're enthusiastic about the adventures in store. Further, we expect that one of your primary reasons for trekking, rather than just being a tourist in Kathmandu, is to experience the elation and satisfaction that come with the effort expended in getting close to the nature and the people of Nepal.

We hope to provide you with the information you'll need to fulfill your expectations and to make your time in Nepal as wonderful as possible. Therefore, the purpose of this book is

- to assist your trek preparation

- to be a resource guide during your trek

- to be a light-hearted travel companion for the rare rainy days in the tent

- to increase awareness of the culture and problems of Nepal

- to be a joyful reminder of the uniqueness of your trip.

What This Book Will Not Tell You

Since many fine books about Nepal are available already, you should check elsewhere for information on

- Nepal visa and immunization requirements

- choosing your trek route and destination

- the ten Nepali phrases most needed by trekkers

- Nepal architecture, history, and ritual beliefs

- where to purchase ceremonial trumpets, and

• flight schedules for Royal Nepal Airlines (RNAC). (Unfortunately, RNAC has difficulty with this one, too.)

Perhaps the most comprehensive, general travel guide available is *Insight Guide: Nepal* (Apa Productions, $16.95), available at most bookstores. It includes not only the specifics required to arrange a trip to Nepal, but also excellent sections on the country's diverse cultures and geography, plus great color photographs to whet your appetite.

For trekking specifics (e.g., how far it is to the next lodge), probably the best book is *A Guide to Trekking in Nepal* by Stephen Bezruchka (The Mountaineers, $10.95). The amount of detail on myriad trek routes is almost overwhelming.

What This Book Will Tell You

Nepal is one of the most exciting and dramatically scenic countries on earth. It can also be one of the most uniquely confusing, frustrating, and outrageous places to visit. With all these elements, it's little wonder that Nepal has become such a popular place for tourists from all over the world—and that a trek has become a highly desirable experience among travelers who want more than a Club Med on the beach.

Information is the key to avoiding a lot of the confusion and frustration possible in Nepal. This book will tell you

• what it's like to go on a trek
• how to care for yourself and stay healthy
• how to look after Nepal's environment and culture
• how to handle unique, foreign situations, and
• how to have a wonderful time!

Nepal is slowly, in its own way, becoming more "modern." But as it surely changes, it nevertheless maintains its own exotic vibrancy and charm. We hope this book will help you discover the vibrancy—and preserve the charm.

What Does It Mean to Trek in Nepal?

Basically, trekking in Nepal means "walking around in the hills." It also means making a commitment to an adventure—a commitment that you should not make lightly.

Nepal blends spectacular natural surroundings with diverse, unique cultures. In Nepal, unlike other parts of the world, it's easy to hire someone who will gladly carry all your stuff, cook all your meals, wash the dishes, and look after you while you trek. There are, however, some important points you should consider to ensure you have the kind of vacation you want.

First, you need to think seriously about why you want to trek and what kind of trek to take. The type of adventure you choose should be in direct proportion to the amount of knowledge and experience you already have.

Trekking in Nepal requires good health, stamina, and fair measures of humor and common sense. While most visitors come prepared in the first three categories, our experience proves that Western definitions of "common sense" aren't always adequate for the Himalayas. This book will provide the realistic information necessary for a rich and safe trekking experience.

Where Do You Want to Go?

Nepal has three geographic zones: the high Himalayan mountains in the north, the lush middle hills and valleys in the center, and the generally hot Terai lowland in the south. While trekking really is only "walking around in the hills," it makes a great deal of difference which hills

11

you decide to walk around in, and which season you'll be walking.

For example, if you're especially interested in seeing the snow peaks, you can see them up close from the highest snow fields and passes, or from the distance of the middle hills (which don't involve the extreme elevations), or even from the back of an elephant walking through the tall grass in the Terai. You have a number of choices, and many people do some of all three—kind of the "Nepal Sampler" approach. An honest evaluation of what you want, of how much experience you've had hiking and backpacking, and of how prepared you are to confront the realities of the adventure will help you make the right choice.

Ask yourself some questions: How ready am I for extended physical exertion? How well do I cope with extremes of weather? How well do I cope with illness? How adaptable am I to changing my plans? And most important of all: What is my real motivation for trekking? Ambition—the need to accomplish a set goal—is the biggest single danger in trekking. People who are willing to remain flexible, who have set reasonable goals but can change them, leave Nepal the most satisfied and the most healthy.

Trekking in Nepal is "walking around in the hills," but it's not like backpacking and camping in other countries. There are no "tourist aid stations" strategically located along the trail. Accept that you'll be far from modern civilization, and prepare to be self-reliant if things go wrong. While trekking in Nepal is not necessarily more dangerous than hiking elsewhere, it is very different.

As the number of trekkers increases, so will the number of accidents. Out of nearly 150,000 trekking tourists per year, there are, on average, only five trekking fatalities. Trekkers could avoid many mishaps if they knew the realities of trekking before their departure. The mountains of Nepal are lovely wilderness almost totally isolated from the amenities and securities of civilization. Lovely—but not inherently kind to strangers.

On the other hand, the mountains are not all wilderness: they are someone's home. Often you'll be walking on a mountain trail that suddenly becomes the village

Main Street. The path may meander beside rice paddies, traverse garden plots, and pass within a few feet of someone's front door. All along the way, you will meet Nepalis and travel within their daily spheres of activity. Our Western minds consider such activity "trespass." To Nepalis, these routes belong to everyone, and they conduct life's daily events in the open, for all passersby to see.

Of course, Nepalis do have concepts of privacy, which you should respect. But, mostly, you are free to come and go as you wish, to stop and observe, or even participate. Since trails are not marked, and since maps are often distorted or inaccurate, you'll have many opportunities to chat and be thankful for all the kind people around. The villagers along the way can be so friendly and courteous that they may say anything to please you. Occasionally, they may even point you in the wrong direction or say that you are very near your destination, simply because you look so tired! For as long you are there, they will treat you as their guest.

Unfortunately, Nepal currently suffers from many forms of ecological stress: deforestation, soil erosion, riversilting, over-population, and, most important for you, the over-development of some popular trekking areas. All of these factors are the realities of trekking. All of these, to some degree, are issues which you, as a trekker, will confront, and they are things to consider while you're making your plans and enjoying your trek.

One of the more important decisions will be to determine just where you want to go and then get an area-specific **Trek Permit** from the Immigration Office, Dilli Bazaar, Kathmandu. (Trekking agency personnel will help you with this bureaucratic detail.) Nepal offers many possibilities, some of which you may have already studied. If you want to see the most spectacular views of the high Himalaya, you'll have to go on the more well-trodden paths, and you'll meet plenty of trekkers along your route. This itself can be an interesting international experience. If you prefer more solitude, you'll need to invest additional preparation time and perhaps a bit more money, and you may have to sacrifice a visit to the "showplaces." But since there's no shortage of scenery in Nepal, the excitement of being off-the-beaten-track and still surrounded by dramatic beauty is worth the effort.

Some Considerations

The most important aspects to consider when choosing a trek destination are your own (or your group's) interests and needs. Some people prefer as much comfort as possible; others enjoy roughing it. A trek with enthusiastic children or seniors can't follow the same route as a trek with high altitude rock-climbers or the super-fit. Some photographers seek broad vistas and beautiful flowers; others prefer village life and interesting faces. Nepal offers it all, but finances, time, and fitness considerations should determine just what you'll do.

The first-time trekker may think that there's an awful lot to consider just for a vacation, and that it may be a bit risky. While these concerns are realistic, this book should encourage and assist you in having a wonderful trekking experience, as simply and safely as possible. Keep in mind that the first trekkers came to Nepal in the 1950's, well before the current trekking service industry began. They were four American women, all over 50.

The only absolute rule in trekking is that you should not go alone. Even on the major routes, it's wise to have someone with you who knows you and your special needs. Many people come to Nepal with friends or family, while others team up with like-minded souls en route. Either of these arrangements can work well. But, just as your trekking style and route involve commitment, so does trekking with others. Once you've formed a group and set reasonable goals, you must confront some serious issues other than amiability. We'll discuss most of these issues in the chapters related to health and safety. For now, your commitment to a trekking experience is the issue, and that commitment brings a large dose of responsibility.

Professional Help

Regardless of who your partners are and where you've decided to go, we urge you to hire people who make it their business to know about trekking. Their services come in many varieties and price brackets.

At one extreme are the full-service, international trekking agencies with tantalizing, glossy catalogs, such as

Wilderness Travel, Overseas Adventure Travel, Narayan's Gateway to Nepal, and InnerAsia Expeditions (addresses and phone numbers below). Look in *Backpacker* and *Outside* magazines for ads for similar outfits. These agencies offer package tours which include all but personal expenses, and you can be confident that a knowledgeable staff and English-speaking guides will handle you and your travel plans well. In general, prices range from $50-$100 per day.

In the middle range, agencies in Kathmandu—such as Mountain Travel, Yeti Travels, Trans Himalaya, Summit Hotel Trekking, and Yager Mountain Guide Services—provide more of a pay-as-you-go service, where you can shop around for what you want and design your own itinerary when you arrive in Nepal. There are dozens of such operations, with varying reputations. Always shop around thoroughly and ask experienced trekkers for their recommendations. In general, you'll get what you pay for. Prices range from $25-$50 per day.

The lowest-priced alternative is the independent Nepali porter/guide whom you hire yourself. There are a number of ways to locate such people, and they may even approach you at the airport or on the street. Generally, it's better to negotiate for such a guide through one of the trekking supply shops located in the Thamel and Freak Street areas of Kathmandu, or through word-of-mouth recommendations. These guides, who operate independent of the larger agencies, provide similar services in procuring equipment, purchasing supplies, organizing transportation (generally by public, long distance buses), and hiring any necessary porters (often family members). They tend to be multi-purpose guides: they know the routes and ideal camping places, and they also "cook and carry." Remember, though, that the services an independent guide provides are the most basic.

One big problem with an independent guide is language. Their proficiency in English can vary greatly, and, initially, it can be difficult to assess their level of comprehension. The major problem in hiring such a guide, however, is reliability. While there are many excellent independent trekking guides, you really have no way to know how good yours will be until you get on the trail.

An independent trek is definitely less expensive. The difference is one of convenience, like going to the super- market and purchasing everything necessary to prepare a meal, including the pots, pans, and dishes, or eating the same meal in a restaurant. Prices for independent treks range from $15-$25 per day. (If you decide to go with an independent guide, we highly recommend Pasang Lama [GPO Box 1802, Kathmandu], an outstanding guide and a wonderful friend.)

Whatever you choose and regardless of your trekking style, this book should prove valuable. Even if you're do- ing a "top-of-the-line" trek, you may find it helpful to know about all the things being done for you, as well as the practical information for your daily routine. It could save you from asking a lot of trivial questions, and it might sug- gest more interesting and relevant topics.

Trekking is a fabulously exciting adventure. It's the kind of experience which often begins with simple curiosity and ends with a commitment well-tempered with love.

Addresses of Companies Mentioned Above

Wilderness Travel
1760 Solano Ave.
Berkeley, CA 94707
800-247-6700
415-524-5111

Overseas Adventure Travel
349 Broadway
Cambridge, MA 02139
800-221-0814
617-876-0533

Narayan's Gateway to Nepal
948 Pearl St.
Boulder, CO 80302
303-440-0331

InnerAsia Expeditions
2627 Lombard St.
San Francisco, CA 94123
800-551-1769
415-922-0448

Mountain Travel Ltd.
GPO Box 170
Naxal, Kathmandu
Phone: 414-508

Yeti Travels Ltd.
GPO Box 76
Durbar Marg, Kathmandu
Phone: 221-234

Trans Himalayan Tours
GPO Box 283
Durbar Marg, Kathmandu
Phone: 223-871

Yager Mountain Guide Service
GPO Box 3968
Bansbari, Kathmandu
Phone: 411-066

Summit Hotel Trekking
GPO Box 1406
Kupondole Heights, Kathmandu
Phone: 521-894

A Trekker's View of Nepal

Trekkers come from all over the world and have diverse backgrounds, interests, and knowledge about Nepal. For some, a trek is only a small part of their itinerary. For others, it's the primary purpose of their trip. Many people read everything they can find about Nepal's history, culture, government, and environment, while others take a "wait and see" approach. Most people find some middle ground between scholarship and serendipity.

Kathmandu, with its government buildings, palaces, temples, cultural activities, and museums, is very different from the hills, where history and infrastructure are less conspicuous and a trekker needs knowledge and a sharp eye to recognize them. Trekking can be more than spectacular scenery. It can be an opportunity to observe tradition and change. It is a chance to understand progress—its process and problems.

This section attempts to describe the "institutions" of Nepal from the point of view of a trekker passing by, observing, and glimpsing what lies behind the obvious. While some detailed information is contained in other sections of the book, people with specific interests should consult more complete sources (see *Further Reading*).

The Environment

Nepal is a land-locked country a little larger than England, wedged between India and Tibet (China). Five hundred miles of Himalaya mountains form the entire northern border. The mountains influence Nepal's climate and

17

economy, and for centuries they have been an obstacle to both people and ideas.

The Himalaya (a word derived from Sanskrit meaning "Abode of the Snows") reflect the diversity of the country they protect. For example, most Nepalis call the highest peak *Sagarmatha*, "The Brow of the Oceans." The Sherpas of eastern Nepal call it *Chomolungma*, Tibetan for "Mother Goddess of the World." To Westerners, it's Mt. Everest, named for the first British official to map the area in 1841.

Nepal's many rivers carry the Himalaya's abundant melting snow south. The water flows first through the harsh mountainous terrain covering the northern third of the country and then through the more temperate middle zone. By the time the run-off reaches the Terai, the flat tropical area in the south, it has formed mighty rivers, including the headwaters of the Ganges, the sacred river of India.

Because the water runs from north to south, any east-west travel in the northern mountains is an exercise in ups and downs. Fortunately, most trekking routes are circuitous, to take advantage of ridge lines and river valleys.

The remote areas of Nepal—and there are still many—are covered in dense forest, home to many unusual species of flora and fauna. The differences in climate and topography created by the Himalaya have also created a wide spectrum of plants and animals in the different regions of the country, as well as distinct ethnic groups.

History and Government

The history of Nepal is long and complex. Its ancient history is a mixture of the legends of the Hindu, Indo-Aryan, valley people migrating north from India and the Tibeto-Burman, Buddhist, mountain peoples from the north and east. More recent history involved a series of conflicting dynasties and rival kingdoms within the Kathmandu Valley, while the mountain areas remained untouched by the chaos.

The modern history of Nepal began in 1786 with Prithvi Narayan Shah's conquest and unification of the Kathmandu Valley. Nepal's current borders were fixed in the early 1800's, when the Treaty of Friendship was established with the British, then in India. This treaty proved to be so disadvantageous to Nepal that the Nepalese rulers closed the borders to all foreigners and did not reopen them again until 1951. They also developed a deep mistrust of India and fear of its expansionist tendencies. This paranoia is still evident in the "political" time-zone change of 15 minutes when you cross the Indian border.

The 1800's were full of palace intrigue and assassinations, as the Rana factions vied for power through the army and the offices of the prime minister. Eventually, the Shah kings became prisoners in their own palaces, and the Ranas ruled for a century.

The Rana prime ministers traveled abroad and returned to "modernize" some traditional Nepal institutions. They started a newspaper, opened schools (even for women), and brought neo-classical ideas, fashion, and architecture to Kathmandu. They did little for the rest of the country, however, and the lives of the rural people remained unchanged.

Following World War II, a liberal Rana proposed a Constitution, the precursor to the current form of government, the parliamentary Panchayat system. The exiled King Tribhuvan, grandfather of King Birendra Bir Bikramn Shah Dev, returned from exile and unseated the last of the Ranas in power.

Today, political activists protest the King's direct authority and control of the partyless Panchayat system. However, the people voted against a multi-party system in 1980—in part because of the traditional belief that the King is the incarnation of the Hindu deity Vishnu. Despite elections, the monarchy is strong, while democratic principles spread. In a recent national election, HMG (His Majesty's Government) proudly announced that, for the first time, no citizen would have to walk more than three days to vote.

As a trekker in the hills outside of Kathmandu, how much evidence of national history and government are you likely to see? Not much. The most obvious governmental arm will be the checkpoints where you must register your trek permit before you can proceed. There are district Panchayat offices, sometimes located by a branch bank. Both usually are closed. If an election is near, you may see handbills and small posters, often with symbols such as eyeglasses, bicycles, or birds to represent different candidates for the illiterate voting population. The further you are from the major population centers, the less "government" you will see. Many villagers do not even know they live in Nepal. To them, Nepal is Kathmandu.

Religion

Nepal's religion is an interesting mixture of Hinduism and Buddhism—the former most pure and strongest in the southern areas, and the latter more prominent in the mountains. Everywhere, except perhaps in Kathmandu Valley, there are also remnants of animistic religions, and practices differ from region to region.

Once out of Kathmandu, religion is more subtle to the casual observer. You will continue to see the red *tika* mark on peoples' foreheads and come upon temples and shrines for worship (*puja*). You may also see Buddhist *mani* walls made of individually inscribed stones left by passing pilgrims. Most houses contain ritual objects, and many people wear amulets around their necks.

In the mountains, people believe that religion has a direct influence on the health and prosperity of people and agriculture, as well as future reincarnations. Practices and traditions vary from group to group. Even if you don't see much physical evidence of religion, you can be sure that it is present and extremely important.

Ethnic Groups

There are 36 dialects spoken in Nepal, although Nepali is the national language and taught in all schools. Many Nepalis speak three or four dialects. In Kathmandu, English is also used extensively.

Ethnic groups tend to divide by region and occupation. It can be quite complicated, as the Hindu caste system is also occupation-based: **Brahmins**, the traditional

Pass to the left: a mani *wall at Lamjung.*

priestly caste; **Chhetris**, the warrior caste; plus numerous lower craftsmen castes. Nepalis, however, do not accept any prohibitions surrounding an ''untouchable'' caste. Many do not subscribe to caste at all, although they do practice some form of the Hindu religion.

The **Newars** predominate in the Kathmandu Valley, where they are the traditional craftsmen, merchants, and civil servants. The women are easily identified by their black saris bordered in red. The Newars have their own caste system, somewhat different from the standard Hindu hierarchy, and they have their own language, still widely used in commerce.

Located in central and western Nepal, **Magars** are usually farmers and shepherds. Their homes are traditionally round or oval shaped. They are strongly influenced by Hinduism and have their own language.

The **Gurungs** also live in central Nepal, although they generally live at higher altitudes than the Magars. They tend to be farmers and shepherds and are starting to succeed as merchants in the Pokhara area. The Gurungs are famous as Gurkha soldiers who have fought for the British and are stationed all over the world. Gurkha regiments attract many young men of the *Chhetri* caste and earn much needed foreign currency for the country. The Gurungs in the high hills are Buddhists, and many still practice traditional shamanism.

You will likely meet **Thakalis** in central Nepal as well. They tend to be successful in business and often own and operate teashops and roadside restaurants frequented by travelers. Known as aggressive traders, they are traditionally the middlemen along the rice-for-salt trade route to Tibet.

The **Kirantis** are the *Rai* and *Limbu* groups of eastern Nepal. They are farmers and shepherds and weave the felt-like blankets and clothing found in the Kathmandu bazaars.

The **Tamangs** are a large and widely dispersed mountain group with a strong Tibetan Buddhist tradition. Many of your porters are likely to be Tamangs who work as day laborers when they are not farming.

Perhaps the best known ethnic group, the **Sherpas** of the eastern Solu-Khumbu region near Everest, are high altitude climbers and guides. They speak a Tibetan dialect and wear traditional Tibetan clothes. Believed to be the most recent migrants to Nepal, they are high country farmers and herders of the famous Himalayan yak.

The **Bhotia** groups are varied, but all live in the most northern regions of the country. They include the *Lopa* and *Manangbas* of the Dhaulagiri and Annapurna regions. They are strongly influenced by their Tibetan origins and culture. Many work as itinerant merchants in villages and along the trails. They also do a thriving business in souvenirs in the Thamel section of Kathmandu.

Tharus, traditional Hindus, live only on the southern Indian border. They are predominantly farmers who live in spacious clay and bamboo houses, often decorated with fish and animal symbols.

As your trek proceeds, you'll almost certainly pass through a number of different ethnic areas, and you may see sub-groups within a single area. While there are physical differences between groups, the variations generally are not apparent along a single trek route. If you have an exceptionally good ear, however, you may pick up dialectic differences. Architectural styles and even the design of simple tools change from village to village, and clothing and women's jewelry are always obvious clues in identifying different ethnic groups along the way.

Art and Crafts

All art in Nepal is based in religion. The Hindu tradition depicts its many deities in wood, stone, bronze, and, to a lesser extent, painting. Buddhist art is based more in representational symbols than images, though both are found in the Thanka painting medium. Tibetan hand-woven carpets are full of symbols, despite a gradual shift away from the traditional colors and motifs to satisfy less flamboyant Western tastes. In the past, Newars were actually "imported" into Tibet to paint the elaborate murals which comprised the original interiors of many monasteries there, now almost completely destroyed. Today, younger painters are also creating landscape art and portraiture to attract tourist dollars.

Along the major trek routes, you will see many *objets d'art*, "antiques," and traditional artifacts for sale. Despite suspicious authenticity, they are often finely crafted and make interesting and representative souvenirs. Often, the most characteristic and authentic items are ordinary utensils found along your trekking route and in the village bazaars. Cookware in brass and wood, ceremonial objects in bronze, baskets and simple tools abound, and all have artistic merit.

If you are interested in buying something of serious collector or museum quality, be sure to ask about the government's antiquity regulations. Reputable dealers are knowledgable and cautious about these laws, as interest in preserving Nepal's artistic heritage increases.

Music and dance also come from a religious tradition, although Western music is having an influence even in the hills, as more Nepalis purchase imported radios and cassette recorders.

Health and Education

Nepal is one of the poorest and least developed countries in the world, due in part to its general remoteness and its specific topography. While trekking, you will see a lot of bad sanitation and malnutrition, although famine is rare. Everywhere you will encounter people suffering from goiter, tuberculosis, possibly leprosy, and many easily-corrected birth defects.

Nepal suffers from high rates of population growth and infant mortality, and life expectancy is about 40 years. Most doctors live in the major cities, and there is very little understanding of, or resources for, preventive medicine. Sadly, in most of Nepal illness is accepted as a fact of life—in dramatic contrast to our assumption that good health is a fundamental right.

No matter where you trek, at some point you will meet children on their way to and from school. Practice your Nepalese with them, and they will gladly practice their English with you. Every school you see will be the same: dreadfully overcrowded and lacking in the most basic materials. The school day is also short, to allow for what can be a two hour walk one way for many children. For a real education, visit a school in session. Is it any wonder much of the rural population is illiterate?

Economy and Agriculture

Nepal has limited natural resources, and with only 14% of its land area suitable for agriculture, it's not surprising that it's so poor. In the hills, where most people farm and raise animals, the per capita cash income in less than $100 a year.

Traditional manufacturing is limited to textiles, leather goods, bricks, cigarettes, matches, and soap, although the availability of cheap labor is starting to bring foreign industry. Nepal earns money by exporting hydroelectric power to India, even though most of the country remains in the dark. (It wasn't until 1982 that Kathmandu had reliable 24-hour electricity.)

Tourism and the sale of permits for major mountain climbing expeditions account for a lot of foreign revenue, too.

Foreign Aid and Technology

Foreign aid and government programs are bringing improvements to rural Nepal. As a member of the Council of Nonaligned Nations, Nepal receives foreign aid and assistance from over 70 countries. You'll probably see many of these efforts, large and small, on your trek: Chinese roads, Swiss dairy and reforestation projects, American bridges and dams, Israeli and British irrigation systems, and the work of Peace Corps volunteers from the USA and Japan. Things are happening all over the country, as numerous organizations tackle malnutrition, sanitation, family planning, education, and economic development.

News and Tourist Information

When the Canadians established a satellite system and trained technicians to operate it in the mid-1980's, communication between Nepal and the outside world improved dramatically. It is now possible to make an international phone call, and the recent arrival of television has brought more international news.

Short wave radio brings in the BBC and Voice of America, as well as a strong signal from Radio Moscow's English language broadcast (interesting listening).

The *Rising Nepal* is an English language newspaper which, alas, has modernized its daily weather forecast. In years past, it was probably the most accurate in the world and especially popular with optimistic trekkers: "Partly cloudy throughout the Kingdom." Progress is indeed a mixed blessing.

International newspapers and magazines are available, though they may not be up-to-the-minute. We've heard a rumor, however, that USA *Today* is now sold on street corners.

There are also free weekly publications, like *Nepal Traveller*, designed for tourists. They usually include a map of Kathmandu and plenty of information about local events, festivals, businesses, and services available to assist you.

How To Do It: Teashops or Tents?

Before you start investigating agencies and routes, you must answer a simple question: Do you want to camp-out and sleep in a tent, or would you rather stay in lodges and teashops strategically located along the trail? Or, do you want to try some of both?

It's not just a question of "Where will I sleep?" The answer will determine the pre-trek preparations you need to make.

Tenting

If you prefer to camp-out, we urge you to hire an agency. They will supply the necessary equipment and are experienced in making all the arrangements, which would be time-consuming and complicated for you to do yourself. They also usually provide ground transportation and include an orientation talk prior to departure.

Agency treks vary greatly in the degree of luxury they provide, so don't assume they will be expensive. Also, by hiring an agency, you'll give yourself the freedom to explore and enjoy Kathmandu Valley before your trek begins, rather than spending your time hunting for supplies and equipment all over town. Agency guides are accountable to their employers, and the agencies carry the required insurance for their people.

Alternately, if you decide to arrange an independent tenting trek, you can rent just about everything you need, as well as a guide, from the trekking supply shops. For more information about the equipment available, refer to the *Equipment and Clothing* chapter.

Trekkers' lodge, Lete.

The Teashop Experience

Teashops are small, family-operated inns which offer meals and sleeping space at a very reasonable cost, and they will give you an entirely different trekking experience than camping. A teashop trek involves far less logistical preparation than camping, and it's a very popular way to go. Teashop treks can be arranged in advance by Force 10 Expeditions (PO Box 547, New Canaan, CT, 06840, phone 800-888-9400 or 203-966-2691).

This comparison chart will give you an idea of the differences between camping and "teashopping."

Teashopping

Advantages	Disadvantages
If you have limited time, there's little preparation required	You can never be quite sure what you'll find when you get there.
You can travel light or hire a porter to carry your belongings.	You carry everything, or you must look after and deal with your porter.
Your accommodations are already set up.	Teashops are usually available only on the more popular routes.
Food and lodging provided	Monotonous menu, health precautions suspect, smoky atmosphere, possible bedbugs
Social opportunities—a chance to meet people from all over the world	Little privacy, less than in genuine Nepali culture
Stereo music, nightlife, electricity	Noisy, definitely not an "outside under the stars" experience
Showers and toilets provided	What you see is what you get!

Tenting

Advantages	Disadvantages
Self-sufficiency—you can go anywhere	You must hire an agency or guide service, or make all the preparations yourself.
Solitude, close to nature and the "real" Nepal	Need to be prepared for being both isolated and the "circus" that comes to town
Close contact with Nepali team/staff	Uncertainties which arise from your role as *sahib* (high-status person in a position of authority)
Increased flexibility in daily itinerary	More daily decision-making required
Opportunity to enjoy impromptu local festivals/happenings	Possibility of becoming lost

Whichever you decide is right for you, you will have a unique experience and a real adventure. Think it through, but remember: some advance preparations are always necessary to ensure that you don't get more adventure than you bargained for.

The 20th Century Comes to Nepal

As you fly into Kathmandu aboard a modern jetliner, you'll immediately be struck by the almost fairy-tale quality of your surroundings. The great painted eyes of the Bodhanath *stupa* watch your descent above a patchwork of fields planted in rice or mustard. There are no skyscrapers, highways, or urban sprawl.

Instead, you'll be greeted by terraced hillsides with pencil-line footpaths that climb to the valley's rim, and on a clear day, the snow-covered Langtang Himalayas stare down from the north. Look closely as you land and you'll see men working their fields with simple plows drawn by water buffalo, pumpkins growing on the roofs of small clay houses, and people on bicycles waiting to pedal across the airport runway.

From the airport, your next stop will be downtown Kathmandu, a short distance away. In the next few days as you wander around the city, you'll be surprised by the juxtaposition of old and new. Ancient, intricately carved temples are surrounded by worshippers as well as vegetable vendors and women laying out their laundry on the sacred steps. You may see a man carrying a full-sized refrigerator on his back, making his way down a busy street past a Mercedes-Benz and pack of roaring Suzuki motorcycles.

Kathmandu has a veneer of the cosmopolitan, but as you become more adventuresome and begin to explore the city away from the comfort of the tourist areas, you'll also see barefoot women pumping water from public wells into polished brass jugs, or washing their kids outdoors in the sunshine, surrounded by the neighborhood dogs and chickens.

Don't be fooled by the designer jeans and video stores. Instead, poke your head into the little manufacturing shops scattered throughout the city—a bicycle shop in Asan Tole or the printer behind the plaza near Hanuman Dhoka. This is the real Kathmandu: labor intensive and technologically simple, people conducting their business in a traditional, "unsophisticated" manner.

Many foreign governments and private development groups currently work in Nepal to assist the country and its people toward a more modern way of life. Some trekkers think projects like road construction and electrification are actually spoiling the country. But whether the changes are beneficial or successful is not for us to discuss in this book. Many interesting things are happening all over the country, and you're likely to see evidence of this modernization in your travels. Check them out—you may be surprised by what you see. We'll let you form your own opinions.

The Impact of You

This chapter is about you, the foreign visitor, and the aspects of modernization that trekkers bring with them and then leave behind.

Nepalis are friendly, curious, and quick to observe differences. You might begin to think, though, that every Nepali you meet is interested only in your money or what you're willing to give away. Nepalis know a lot about—and desire—expensive, Western products. But few Nepalis can afford many of the things you take for granted. The average trekker carries more wealth in cash and equipment than the average Nepali can earn (let alone save) in a year. Physical assaults and theft, although infrequent, do occur.

The best prevention: diminish temptation. Keep your camera, jewelry, and extra money deep inside your luggage and out of sight as much as possible. Keep only small bills in your pocket or wallet. If you're camping, you can hire someone or assign one of your team as a night guard.

Even then, store your valuables in the middle of your tent, not in the corners (where tent-slashers may strike), and never leave things outside overnight.

You must also be careful if you're staying in teashops. Although your valuables are less accessible to poor Nepali villagers, you are vulnerable to theft by other trekkers. Always secure your valuables as best you can (many people use small luggage locks). Never leave your gear unattended.

The "free and easy" interpersonal and sexual behaviors of foreigners can confuse traditional Nepalis. Women should be aware that their manner of dress may be viewed as "undress" by local men—and be seriously misinterpreted. Shorts and halter tops are not compatible with Nepali customs regarding physical modesty and morality. Pay attention to the nonverbal messages you send.

Trekkers, as much as any development program, are "agents of change," and their behavior has an impact. Nepalis have learned a great deal from their visitors, and some of this new information is having a negative effect.

The most dramatic evidence of this, sadly, is the growing problem of drug addiction among Nepali youth.

Many trekkers come to Nepal with a high level of Western paranoia. It's neither appropriate nor necessary. Nepalis are generally honest and sincerely warm and friendly. All you really need is good old common sense. Give yourself, and the Nepalis you meet, a fair chance—''innocent until proven guilty''—and then relax and enjoy the unique openness of this fascinating, changing culture.

Residents of Landrung.

A Bit
About Food

Trekkers tend to think about food a lot. Of course, once you're underway, there's not much you can do about it. If you didn't give enough thought to your meals beforehand, you're stuck with what you've got.

If you're trekking with an agency, they will plan your meals for you, and they might even give you a menu. Agencies have a lot of experience preparing food for trekkers, and they provide a variety of palatable meals, properly (read, hygienically) prepared and served with relative elegance. You won't need to dress for dinner, however.

The trekkers' daily fare contains more carbohydrates than you would normally eat in a week: plenty of oatmeal, porridge, and pancakes (with honey), flat bread *chapatis* with peanut butter and (gasp) jam, noodles, mountains of rice and potatoes, as well as the ubiquitous glucose cookies that appear whenever tea is served.

If you are lucky you may even get cake—baked in a flat-bottomed *dekshi* over an open campfire. While it poses no threat to Duncan Hines, it is a pleasant change from pudding. Of course there are eggs—yes, one of the porters will be carrying a wire basket with enough fresh (?) eggs for your entire trek—and plenty of cheese, salami, cauliflower, and green leafy vegetables, generically named *sag*. If someone has recently slaughtered a goat or water buffalo in a village you pass through, you may be eating it for dinner that night. Chickens are often bought and butchered en route, but they are not the tender, succulent kind that come wrapped in plastic. These birds, too, spend a lot of time on their feet.

The basic Nepali diet is mainly vegetarian—animal protein is primarily festival food—consisting of *baht* (rice), *dahl* (cooked lentils), and *takari* (a mild curry of whatever vegetables are in season, generally overcooked). Nepal is not a country of haute cuisine, but the nutritional value of *dahl/baht/takari* is excellent, and you'll find that it's a very satisfying meal, ideal for trekking appetites. Experienced trekkers often prefer it to the campsite attempts at Western Variety. Your palate must wait for wonderful, inexpensive, international foods until you return to Kathmandu.

Whenever possible, your guides will include fresh apples, bananas, and oranges, as well as dried fruit brought from Kathmandu. Fruit is perfectly safe to eat, but remember to peel the apples first.

If you are teashopping, you will decide where, when, and what to eat. All the teashop menus tend to look alike and are limited to what is locally available (meat, vegetables, rice, noodles) supplemented with whatever has been carried in (jam, custard, milk, beer, and soft drinks). Teashop proprietors have become quite adept at satisfying Western tastes and can create especially enticing variations on desserts. Even trekkers with agencies have been known to stop at a teashop for a delicious piece of apple pie.

Independent trekkers have the option of enjoying both: they can plan to eat some meals in teashops and still enjoy *al fresco* dining elsewhere. If you're planning an independent trek, you'll need to know what's available along your route. At various times, the government designates some regions of Nepal "Food Deficit Areas," and it's very unwise to assume that you can live off the land. We urge you to do your homework before leaving Kathmandu and to seek the assistance of a guide/cook when deciding what and how much to buy. Novice trekkers often miscalculate how much they'll be eating—it's more than they eat normally, for sure. Plus, you are responsible for feeding your Nepali team, who generally prefer their staple *dahl/baht/takari*.

A Note to Weight-Watchers

It's common to think of trekking as an ideal opportunity to loose extra pounds. With all the additional exercise and the absence of so many tempting delights, it should be a cinch to loose weight, right?

Wrong! Dieting on the trail is not a good idea, and our experience shows that it doesn't work, anyway.

To maintain your health and energy, you'll require a substantial quantity of food, and you'll probably find yourself eating more, not less. (Perish the thought!) Your appetite will keep pace with your increased level of exercise. You'll probably finish your trek healthier and stronger—but about the same weight as when you left.

The optimal diet for trekking contains a high level of carbohydrates and as much liquid as possible. Soups are an excellent way to increase fluid intake and feed a hungry body. Although most Westerners aren't accustomed to eating large quantities of rice, noodles, and potatoes, they are the best trekking food. They can be supplemented with fruit when available and vitamins, if you're so inclined. Also, stock up on high-energy snacks—dried fruits, nuts, granola, and chocolate—for munching along the way. Besides giving a little power-boost at the bottom of a long ascent, such snacks help people avoid over-eating at meals and the dreadful feeling that follows such indulgence.

One of the real joys of trekking is to finally take off your pack, sit down with your feet up (but not pointing at anyone—a serious taboo in Nepali culture), and eat a good meal. You'll be surprised how delicious everything tastes!

A Bit
About Money

Unless you're trekking with an agency, you'll need to bring enough money to cover food, lodging, salary for porters and guides, and miscellaneous goodies. Sometimes the larger district branches of the Nepal Rastrya Bank will change foreign currency and travelers' checks, but it's wiser to do the necessary transactions before leaving Kathmandu or Pokhara. Be sure to keep all bank exchange receipts, as you will be allowed to change back only 15% of the total of the official receipts when you leave Nepal.

Since most of your purchases on the trek will be small, carry small denominations: 1, 2, 5, 10, 20 rupee notes. It can be very difficult to get even a Rs. 100 note (approximately $4.00) changed along the way, and it's not a good idea to be flashing large bills.

Get an estimate of probable daily expenses (they'll depend on where you're going and the style of your trek), and calculate accordingly for the number of days you'll be out. Unless you're restricted by a fixed itinerary or time, always assume that you'll be out a few days longer than you think, and get enough cash to cover any delays. Though most of the guidebooks are fairly accurate in the travel times they give, many variables can affect your pace (blisters, weather, illness, tempting hot springs, etc.). Also, prices are rising all over Nepal. The further you get from the population centers, the more expensive everything becomes. Calculating for a few extra days is a good way to cover most contingencies.

About Rs. 150-200 per day should easily cover your

basic food and lodging requirements. If you're doing an independent trek with a porter/guide, be sure to plan for his salary and his meals. Remember, too, that the best financial planning can quickly collapse when you're confronted with a cold Coke on a hot day, or when you decide to buy an extra beer for a new friend.

Keep your wad of money—and it will be a substantial bundle with all those small bills—safe and out of sight. Each morning before you pack up, take out only the cash you think you'll need for the day. Many people use either a money belt or an around-the-neck purse to keep their cash and papers secure. Others like the fanny pack/belly bag; it keeps your money secure, and you don't have to undress to get to it.

If you are unlucky and lose all your money—wallets do fall into rivers and backpacks do get stolen—you'll be forced to rely on the generosity of friends or strangers for loans until you can sort out the mess. If you lose your trekking permit, or worse still, your passport, you're in for a great lesson in patience. You can make few official transactions without the appropriate papers, and the embassies are not always efficient or sympathetic.

We suggest you photocopy your passport, including the photo page and visa pages, to keep with you on the trail. (You can get photocopies made in Kathmandu.) Ask your Kathmandu hotel proprietor or trek shop owner to keep your original passport, extra travelers' checks, and cash in their vault while you are out of town.

Begging and Tipping

Throughout Nepal you will meet beggars—both serious, persistent professionals and playful children who want only "one rupee," a pen, or candy. The very fact that they are in this line of work indicates that they've had past success. How you handle them is your own decision, but keep in mind three general notions:

1. The closer you are to the major tourist attractions, including the big Kathmandu hotels on Durbar Marg, the larger the crowds of beggars become, and the less needy the beggars actually are.

2. In the culture of Nepal, one can gain merit by giving to beggars. But in the beggars' minds, you are just plain rich and an easy touch.

3. There is dignity in work, even menial work by Western standards, and it's perfectly acceptable to pay people for even the smallest services.

Beggars can be most annoying. It helps to remind yourself that most people, no matter what nationality, will gladly accept something for nothing. Also, even the poorest people, no matter what nationality, have some pride. You'll have to decide how you want to deal with them, but a smile never complicated the situation.

Tipping, a Western concept, is quickly gaining popularity in Nepal. The further you are from areas frequented by foreigners, the lower the expectation for a tip. However, you should tip Nepalis who accompany you on a trek. The specifics are covered in the chapter about the Nepali crew.

Weather
and Altitude

By latitude, Nepal is located in a sub-tropical zone. But the extremes in elevation—from 492 feet (150 meters) above sea-level in the southern Terai to 29,028 feet (8,825 meters) at the top of Mt. Everest—make Nepal a country where you can experience rapid weather changes in a very short time. Combinations of location, season, altitude, and even time of day can significantly affect the local climate and you as a trekker.

Nepal's climate is characterized by two distinct seasons: the colder, drier wintertime and the hot, humid, rainy summer monsoon. The ideal trekking times are October/November and March/April, when temperatures are moderate and skies are clear. Nevertheless, trekkers come year round to hike in all kinds of weather.

In Kathmandu, late September days are warm, shirt-sleeve weather, as the summer rains taper off to occasional showers. While the nights begin to cool and a jacket is desirable, the skies are clear and the air has a fresh-washed smell that reflects the vibrant greens and golds of the autumn landscape. It's harvest time, and there's much activity and many festivals.

During October and November, the air becomes more crisp, ideal for the hard, hot work of trekking. The rains have stopped, and the snowy mountains, clearly visible in bright sunlight, at night reflect the eerie glow of the autumn moon. December becomes even colder, with an occasional frost. January days begin in thick fog which normally burns off by 10:00am. The nights are very cold, and the mid-winter monsoon arrives: generally about two weeks of intermittent rain, which is snow in the higher elevations.

By February, as the days lengthen and the daytime temperatures rise, the mountains come into view again. While February and March are cold months for trekking, they are also the time when spectacular red, pink, and white canopies of the rhododendron forests bloom. Of course, spring comes more slowly the higher up you go, and it's not uncommon, even in April, to encounter snowstorms above 15,000 feet (4,560 meters).

By late April, days and nights are quite warm again. Since there's been no rain for many months, the air becomes dusty and heavy with rising humidity, which precedes the summer monsoon. The rainy season begins with heavy afternoon showers in May.

During the summer monsoon months (June to September), mornings are clear and warm with bright sunshine. As the day progresses, the air becomes more humid, and beautiful monsoon clouds billow like skyscrapers overhead against a brilliant blue sky. The heavy rains at 4:00pm, which lasted only an hour in May, now continue into the early evening.

By August, it's raining almost every night. Often these evening torrents are accompanied by spectacular thunder and lightning shows. It rains all day only at the very end of the monsoon.

Many people actually enjoy trekking during the monsoon, particularly to the Kaligandaki area where it is dry year round. There are fewer travelers on the trails, and once you develop a tolerance for the forest leeches and pass behind the Annapurna Massive, the monsoon is over.

The Pokhara area (elevation: 3,000 feet, 912 meters) and the Terai are lower, so their weather tends to be warmer than the above description of the central Kathmandu Valley region (4,368 feet, 1326 meters). Trekking out of Pokhara, even in the winter months, is hot work indeed, until you reach the higher elevations.

Many problems result from incomplete knowledge of the climate. At higher elevations, the temperature can fluctuate as much as 60° Fahrenheit (33° centigrade) in a single day. You must prepare for extremes, and you

Tibetan traders near Tukche.

should always inquire about probable weather conditions before setting off into remote areas. Agency personnel know the weather and how much snow is in the high passes. If they're not taking people into a region at a particular time of year, there's a good reason for it! Before you commit yourself to a specific destination, find out what the weather will be like, and then decide if you're prepared for it.

Equipment and Clothing

You can buy or rent everything you need for a successful trek in Kathmandu. Pre-paid agency treks supply lists of what their packages provide, and the local trekking agencies—there will be one either in the lobby of your hotel or very nearby—can direct you to the rental shops, primarily in the Thamel and Freak Street areas of Kathmandu. There's no need to overload your luggage with sleeping bags and mats, ground sheets and gaiters. Most people like to have their own boots and clothing, although you can rent or buy down jackets and even wool socks in Kathmandu.

The equipment available, far more in Kathmandu than in Pokhara, is the left-overs of trekkers who won't be needing thermal underwear in Thailand and the major mountain climbing expeditions who aren't funded to ship their used equipment home. Therefore, it's possible to find top-of-the-line gear from all over the world at reasonable prices, as well as the more mundane supplies you'll need.

Boots, the most important piece of equipment, are the most difficult to find. Trekking supply shops prefer to sell outright the newer, lightweight boots, so finding comfortable, correctly fitting boots for rent can be a problem, particularly if your feet are unusually large or small. There are many rental pairs of the older and heavier leather boots, since almost nobody uses them any more.

No matter what you rent, shop around for your equipment, and go to the trouble in the confined and cluttered space of these shops to scrutinize each item before you rent it. While rental costs are quite reasonable (e.g., $2.00-$5.00 per day for a tent), the equipment is used and may not be in great condition. If you discover a broken zipper on your sleeping bag once you're up in the hills, you'll just have to suffer. If a pole is missing from your tent gear, your tent might be useless. Though we've never known trek shop owners who knowingly rent faulty equipment, sometimes errors happen, and a problem will be your headache, not theirs, until you return.

If you rent equipment in Nepal, please take good care of it—the kind of care you would take with your own gear. Nepal is a poor country, and camping equipment represents a sizeable investment. Common sense will prevent most damage. For instance, never light a candle in a tent without the proper container-type lantern, found in the trekking shops. (Besides, a good flashlight is safer and more helpful.)

Rental prices are fairly uniform from one shop to the next, but purchase prices can vary greatly and are negotiable. Remember, whenever you bargain, shop around enough in advance to get the ballpark figures, and then keep the haggling light-hearted. An extra dollar or two means a lot more to a Nepali than to you.

The Basic Clothing List

This list is quite variable and depends on your intended altitude, the season, and personal comfort requirements. Be prepared for anything weather-wise, and don't forget hats, gloves, socks, and possibly long underwear. Always err on the side of dressing for weather that's colder than you expect.

- Two pairs of comfortable long pants. While blue jeans may be your favorite, they aren't warm, they chafe, and they take a long time to dry. Women often prefer skirts or culottes.

- One pair of shorts/swimsuit (or large wrap-around cloth)—anything suitable for bathing in semi-public places.

- Three changes of underwear.

- Four shirts. Choose between t-shirts, short- or long sleeved shirts, cotton or wool, depending on your destination and time of year.

- Three pairs of cotton socks and two pairs of heavy socks. You can wear them in layers, but always have a clean pair next to your feet.

- One warm jacket.

- One pair of rubber sandals for bathing or just airing your feet.

- Two neckerchiefs—nice for absorbing sweat, for washing, and for keeping the sun off the back of your neck.

- Mittens, gloves, hats as needed. Don't forget protection from the sun.

- Sleepwear. Treat yourself to sleeping in something that's not trail-worn, like a fleecy sweatsuit.

- One down vest, down pants, down booties, and gaiters—all are handy extra layers if it gets really cold.

- Two pairs of shoes. Armies march on their stomachs, trekkers on their feet. The most important item of equipment is your shoes. Many people pack soft trekking boots and a pair of running shoes. Whatever you choose, you must have two pairs of comfortable shoes, if for no other reason than to vary the location of your blisters.

For the first few days, as you sweat profusely at the lower elevations, you may wonder why you're carrying all these clothes. But in a few days—and a few thousand feet higher—you may wish you'd brought even more. Even on a warm day, a change in the clouds or the wind can bring cold, rain, or snow by evening. Regardless of the season, you may experience the weather of any other season, so be prepared.

g bag
- ins... ...eping pad
- ground s... et or poncho
- leak-proof water bottle
- reliable flashlight with extra batteries and bulbs
- umbrella for rain or sun
- duffle-type bag (for all those things you need but can't face carrying)

Optional:
- daypack for short trips (or in lieu of a backpack if you're having porters carry everything)
- tent
- matches or cigarette lighters
- maps

Other Useful Items:
- Toiletries: lots of soap, toothbrush and toothpaste, shampoo, washcloth, chapstick, skin lotion, insect repellent, and sunscreen. (It's convenient to put these items in a small, resealable, plastic container, which can double as a portable sink.)
- eating utensils
- toilet paper
- medium sized towel
- Swiss Army knife
- safety pins
- extra shoe laces
- small pair of scissors
- needle and thread
- bungie cords or heavy twine
- assorted sizes of plastic bags
- extra iodine tablets or water purification solution
- whistle (it's great for getting help)
- binoculars
- assorted sizes and colors of stuff sacks (to help keep your stuff dry, clean, and in some sort of order)
- glacier glasses or sunglasses with side shields to block snow glare

- down booties
- deep snow gaiters
- writing paper, books, playing cards, juggling balls, and a ball of string to teach kids Cat's Cradle
- Teddy bear (for those private moments when you're not sure why you did this at all . . .)

At this point, remember—in Nepal you can hire eager porters who will carry everything.

Trekkers' Fashion Tips

Clothes may make the man, but the best dressed trekkers will all be wearing layers this season—and every other season as well.

The principle is very simple: with variable weather conditions, the easiest way to adjust your body temperature is to adjust your clothing. While long underwear may seem essential when you wake on a frosty morning, it'll be too warm by midday when you're working hard on an uphill grade. Making your adjustments from the outside in, rather than the inside out, is not a major change of wardrobe, just a minor alteration.

The Four Basic Layers

The *underwear layer* maintains comfort next to your skin. It provides a minimal degree of thermal insulation, and it should regulate the amount of moisture on the skin. Cotton, wool, or silk absorb moisture well, but polypropylene is best for really cold weather.

The *clothing layer* is both important and versatile. It should absorb moisture, provide thermal insulation, and protect against the elements. The fit of your clothing is very important, too—it shouldn't be either too big, too baggy, or too tight.

The *insulation layer* provides the primary protection against cold. Sweaters, jackets, and vests fall into this category, as well as the heavy-duty down jackets and suits used by high altitude climbers. In general, thickness is a reliable indicator of potential warmth, but even the heaviest down jacket is useless when wet, and down can take days to dry. Synthetic fibers like polyester pile and nylon fleece keep you warm even if they're wet, but they are more bulky than down.

The *outer shell layer* adds additional protection against the harshest elements of wind, rain, and snow. A waterproof jacket and pants can make a big difference. Although you may never use them, you'll be glad you brought them along if the need arises.

Consider your route, and take along a few variations: a wool shirt or sweater, a down vest, and perhaps a nylon/fleece outer jacket. This way, you can vary your layers as the conditions require. Be sure your outer layer garments are large enough to fit over all the other layers you might be wearing underneath.

A Further Note on Footwear

Comfort is the most important thing in footwear, although the tread can also make a big difference. On most trails, you don't need boots with bottoms that look like studded snow tires. However, smooth-bottomed shoes are likely to put you smoothly on your bottom.

Casual footwear, like tennis or jogging shoes, is fine for trekking in the middle hills, but they don't protect against the cold in higher altitudes. One of the most serious and most easily avoidable problems is frostbite, which can result if shoes become wet. One pair of shoes should be light, cool, and quick to dry. The other should be heavier for higher altitudes and for the long, steep, and possibly muddy downhill stretches.

Many people see what the Nepalis wear—rubber sandals or Chinese canvas shoes—and think they can emulate them. But if you look closely, you'll see that all Nepalis who trek for a living have appropriate footwear. If you'll be trekking in the higher elevations, be sure you have proper footwear—and inspect your Nepali team's shoes as well.

Break in your boots as much as possible before you go, and wear them on the plane if you're flying into Nepal.

If the airline loses your bags, you can replace most everything else—except your broken-in, comfortable, user-friendly footwear.

Still Cold?

Your body's rate of metabolism directly affects how warm or cold you are when you sleep. In general, well-conditioned, physically fit people (and folks with more fat or muscle) stay warmer during sleep, but anyone can improve sleeping comfort and warmth with a few simple hints:

• *Drink plenty of water, even in cold weather.* Dehydration can reduce blood circulation, resulting in cold hands and feet, particularly at night. The idea of drinking so much that you'll need to leave your warm sleeping bag in the middle of a cold, windy night is not enticing, but it's important to keep your body hydrated. Not only will you sleep more soundly, but if you do need to go out on a late-night bladder patrol, you'll at least have the stars all to yourself.

• *Sleep on an insulating sleeping mat with a ground sheet under it.* While the comforts of an air mattress are well known to anyone who loves the beach, you don't want one on a trek. True, an air mattress is soft and protects you from rocks and bumps, but it also efficiently transfers your body heat into the ground. It's better to forego the "Princess and the Pea" approach and use a thinner, insulating type of mat. Many provide both warmth and comfort.

• *Go to bed warm.* If you are chilled before you get into your sleeping bag, take a brisk walk around the campsite before retiring. A little exercise works much better than a shot of brandy.

• *Sleep lightly clothed*. When you're really cold, you'll be tempted to climb into your bag with all your clothes on. But it's not the most effective way to warm up quickly, and you're likely to wake up later drenched in sweat. Then you'll have to wiggle out of all those layers and get chilled in the process. It's far more effective to wear a light layer of clothing and let your sleeping bag provide the insulation. Unless your bag is totally inadequate for the conditions, you'll be more comfortable wearing less.

• *Or, sleep naked*. Sleeping in only socks and a hat can make a big difference. Try it! Buy some fuzzy flannel and have a tailor sew it into a long tube for the inside of your sleeping bag. Be sure that it's wide and long enough so you can cuddle it up, particularly around your neck and shoulders. It's much warmer next to your skin than the chilly nylon of most bags, and the liner will keep your bag fresh and clean.

• *Use a hot water bottle*. Before you go to bed, fill your water bottle with boiling water and sleep with it. As long as it doesn't leak, it makes a marvelous companion. Don't use metal canteens, however.

• *Sleep with a friend*. This suggestion is made solely in the interest of conserving body heat. Anything else you choose to make of it is your business. A warm body can heat a cold one quickly. Of course, it's nicer to receive someone else's warmth, but giving and receiving is what companionship is all about. At least talk it over . . . You can buy sleeping bags that can be zipped together to make a "double."

• *Put plastic over your sleeping bag to reduce heat loss and protect against the wind*. Unfortunately, plastic will also increase condensation, and you may wake up sweating. Plastic works, but it's not the best solution.

• *Fluff your sleeping bag*. Often, bags made with down get matted and develop cold spots. Give it a good shake before you lay it out for the night, and check for shifting insulation. Locate your sleeping area out of drafts and winds.

If Your Bag Gets Wet

Down-filled bags lose over 90% of their insulating ability when wet, and they can take two to three days of constant fluffing to thoroughly dry. So keep your bag in a waterproof stuff sack. It's also a good idea to lay it in the sun as much as possible. Lunch breaks often yield a quiet, sunny rest for you and your bag.

Bags with synthetic fibers lose only 10% of their thermal efficiency when wet, and they'll usually drip-dry in less than a day. You can sleep in a wet synthetic bag if you have to, but be sure to have dry clothes to change into in the morning.

It's best to take a bright, sunny rest day if, unhappily, everything gets soaked.

Speaking of wetness: While you're drying your bag, you can also dry your laundry. If you wash those awful socks just before breakfast and pin them to the outside of your pack, they should be ready for a "final cycle" of drying by lunchtime. Lunch is also a great time to wash your hair and feet.

The Packed Pack

Once you've assembled all your clothing and equipment, it's time to pack your bags. Experienced trekkers don't try to carry everything—they hire a porter and put the extras (those "just in case" items) into a duffle bag to be carried for them. Their pack, then, contains only things they'll probably use during a single day's trek, typically one clothing item of each layer and the necessary bits and pieces, like a camera, water purification tablets/drops, toilet paper, etc.

Remember, a backpack that feels "reasonable" while you're standing can become very heavy after hours of walking up and down the hills. Test your weight tolerance by packing your pack with the essentials and taking a half-hour hike around town. Ideally, a four-hour walk is best, but a brief, hilly hike should give you some idea how heavy the pack really is, and how it's riding on your back.

The Weight Should Be on the Hips

Many trekking agencies suggest that a day pack is all you'll need, and, if you consider only carrying capacity for essentials, they're right. A day pack is usually something like a student's book bag, and, while it may be neatly outfitted with little compartments, it isn't designed for comfortable, long distance travel.

You'll be better off with a slightly larger pack (you don't have to fill it) designed to distribute the load efficiently and comfortably, so your shoulders don't do all the work. The weight of your loaded pack should not push down on your shoulders. You should be able to rotate your shoulders freely and slide your hand easily between the strap and your chest. If you can't, adjust the straps.

You also don't want the weight of the pack on your waist. It will be more comfortable if it's carried on your hips. Adjust the hip belt and shoulder straps to get the best feel.

Finally, you don't want to feel as though the pack is pulling you over backwards, or to one side or the other. It should ride squarely and evenly on your hips. If you have problems, check the distribution of weight inside the pack. Put heavy items in the middle near the top, and pad them so they don't bounce around inside.

If you're renting or borrowing a pack, or even using a trusted "old friend," be sure to check for sharp bits of metal protruding from the frame. The jagged edge of a cotter-pin or a bent circle ring can take a large chunk out of your hand or leg. Inspect your pack carefully, and tape over (or file down) anything that seems the least bit hazardous.

Since conditions will change and you'll carry different items as the trek proceeds, adjust your pack frequently. Check for comfort each time you reload, and be prepared to make some choices if you're having trouble carrying all the items you think you need. You'll meet your porter and your duffle bag each evening, so your stuff is accessible, though not instantly. It's a good idea, too, to carry a little less the first few days, until you get accustomed to the routine and the load. Even pack-mules go through a training period.

And remember: always bend your knees when lifting.

Low Impact Trekking: "Leave Only Footprints Behind"

In the past few years, there have been a number of major expeditions to Everest Base Camp, but their purpose has not been to assault the peak. Rather, they went just to clean up all the litter and garbage that other climbers had thoughtlessly, though conveniently, left behind.

Throughout Nepal, littering has become a serious eyesore. Nepalis themselves are uncertain how to deal with it. Traditionally, they just threw their little bits of trash anywhere. But Nepali trash is biodegradable: the vegetable garbage, and even much of the paper, is consumed by animals.

Westerners generally avoid littering in their home countries. But when they get to Nepal, so much garbage is lying around that they tend to relax their standards and "go native." Unfortunately, Western garbage (like that left at Everest Base Camp) won't decompose or be eaten: gas cylinders, broken tent poles, bottles, tin cans, etc.

Whether you are tenting or teashopping, you will have stuff to throw away. You can either burn it, bury it, give it to someone (if it's a container, don't crush or break it; villagers will gladly take it off your hands if it's reusable), or carry it with you until you find an appropriate way to discard it. The point is, **don't leave your garbage lying around**.

Toileting Options

This brings us to toilet practices. Since the local municipalities have not yet installed either rubbish bins or Port-

O-Lets along the trail, improvisation is the key. As in-novative as trekkers are, it's sometimes difficult to find a toilet site that hasn't been used many times before, and you should be considerate of the many who will follow you. Again, we suggest that you choose either the "bury it" or "carry it" options, depending on your personal style in these matters.

It's always unpleasant to discover soiled toilet paper and sanitary napkins when you've found the perfect place at the perfect moment. We always try to find toilet sites with the following characteristics: good cover, good drainage, good footing, and a good view. (After all, if you must stop for a few minutes, you might as well enjoy the view.)

When you finish, consider the others who will also want to enjoy the location, and bury whatever you've left behind. Nepali custom eschews toilet paper for the more basic and economical water and left hand approach. (Therefore, it's considered extremely crude to use your left hand in eating in the company of Nepalis, and be sure to pass plates and even money with your right hand.)

A Quick History Lesson

In some parts of the world where this left-handed system of hygiene has been used for centuries, punishment for convicted criminals was to chop off their right hands. The criminal became an instant social outcast at minimal government expense.

End of lesson.

A Personal Message

To the "Pink Magic Woman" who preceded me from Ghorepani to Ghandrung:

I'm sorry you had such a terrible cold while trekking through this exquisite forest. Though we never met, I hope that some day we both can return to Nepal to en-joy trekking again, and that next time you will be feeling better.

If, however, you again have a head cold and are forced

to blow your nose every five minutes along the trail, please put your used Pink Magic tissues in your pocket or practice the local Pink Magic substitute:

1. Tilt your head slightly forward and in the direction of the obstructed nostril.

2. Inhale deeply.

3. Close the opposite nostril with the index finger of your right hand.

4. Exhale forcefully.

5. Now, take a fresh Pink Magic tissue from your pocket and

6. Wipe off your leg.

7. Return the soiled tissue to your pocket and

8. Bury or burn it later.

Deforestation

Another important aspect to consider while traveling throughout Nepal is deforestation. In the hills of Nepal, the traditional fuel is either wood or manure. Although manure would be more wisely used as fertilizer to enrich the soil, it is dried (that's what those brown pancakes on the sides of houses are) and burned instead. In some locations, Nepalis are using methane gas generation to provide fuel for household cooking and lighting. Should you come upon one of these units in operation, stop and explore; they are quite interesting.

Nevertheless, Nepalis have always preferred wood, and today villagers must travel farther and farther from their homes to collect the needed supplies. Without alternative fuel resources, deforestation will continue. It's a complex issue, but as a trekker, whether teashopping or tenting, you are a part of the problem. Though reforestation efforts are underway, the trees just don't grow fast enough.

In the Annapurna Conservation Area, officials have proposed creating kerosene depot sites and prohibiting tourists from using wood fuel. In the Langtang and Sagarmatha/Everest National Parks, these prohibitions are enforced, and violators receive substantial fines.

An innocent cause of deforestation, Ghandrung.

Regardless of where you are trekking, you must demonstrate concern for the future of the land. If you are teashopping, it's basically out of your hands, but if you are tenting, you can begin to alleviate the problem. Should you decide to use kerosene (and we hope that you will, at least partially), you will create additional preparation concerns. You'll need to arrange for a porter to carry the kerosene, cooker, and replacement parts. Your biggest problem may be to convince your cook to use them. But try!

For high altitude trekking—where wood is unavailable and kerosene is impractical—bottled gas works well and is available in Kathmandu. Remember to bring the empty cylinders with you when you return.

Wherever you are, resist the temptation to sit around that cozy campfire. Instead, try a brisk game of charades by the light of a kerosene lantern to keep warm.

Hiring Your Nepali Crew

For trekking in Nepal, hiring someone else to carry all your gear is hardly a luxury. You can hire a single porter/guide or an entire entourage, depending on your budget and the type of trek experience you want. Since you've already spent a lot of money getting to Nepal, a little bit more can't hurt your pocketbook all that much. If nothing else, think of it as direct foreign aid.

Even the most frugal trekkers are advised to hire someone who can carry most of the gear, speak the language, and smooth the way through the unexpected difficulties that can occur. For those people with more financial flexibility, many agencies exist that can care for you in five-star splendor (tents, chairs, and tables for dining, plus a portable privy), as well as cater to any unique requests (singing porters, perhaps?). Of course, there's a large middle ground in services and prices.

Even if you've purchased a package deal from a travel agent, you should read through this section to understand the job descriptions of the people you'll be dealing with on a daily basis.

Job Specifications

Sirdar: The number one man in your crew will be the *sirdar.* His primary responsibility is to look after you, and he handles all the logistical arrangements of routes, porters, food, and sleeping sites. The *sirdar* also manages the money for on-trail expenses, porters' wages, and transportation charges. If you've hired him through an agency, his English could be quite good, and he may be knowledgeable about local customs and sights.

If you're going on an agency trek, your *sirdar* will have the cash necessary for daily transactions. You'll need money only for personal expenses along the trail and tips/bonuses (*baksheesh*) given at the end of the trek. A good rule-of-thumb for tipping is one extra day's wage for every week out, with more added for exceptional service.

Of course, all of this depends on the length and type of trek as well. Some agency treks include the services of a Western leader, knowledgeable in the culture and fluent in the language. These men and women can assist you with tipping considerations for Nepalis, and most would appreciate tips themselves. Nepalis always appreciate donations of used clothing and gear. Westerners prefer cash!

If you've decided to trek independently, be sure to talk with your *sirdar* directly. While the trekking supply shops can make all the arrangements for you, it's unwise to head into the mountains without some familiarity with your main-man.

Independent *sirdars* work by the day, and they can be paid for extra days to assist with additional tasks like shopping for provisions, choosing rental equipment, obtaining trek permits, etc. They usually request an advance on their salary—the balance payable at the end of the trek—to leave behind with their families. Your *sirdar* will act as paymaster for the rest of your Nepali crew. Remember, the money you carry should be in small denominations.

Be sure to ask around to get information on the going rates, but be aware that there are good reasons—such as destination and length of trek—for variations. You may also have to pay extra if you'll be trekking during a major Nepali holiday, particularly Desain, which occurs in early autumn.

To manage and monitor the money, keep a written record of the amounts you are giving the *sirdar*, and ask for an accounting (by the meal/place/day/purchase—whatever seems appropriate) of how it was spent. There's no way to guarantee complete honesty or precise bookkeeping, but showing an interest, via curiosity, is better than acting like an angry loan officer or IRS investigator later.

Sherpas: Your *sirdar* may also be referred to as a "Sherpa," though this term actually applies to a specific ethnic group, famous for high altitude climbing. Obviously, not all *sirdars* are of Sherpa heritage, and not all Sherpas are *sirdars*. But it never hurts to express an interest in your crew's background, home, and family to establish rapport and learn about the culture.

   A Sherpa is also a guide. In this way, your *sirdar*, although the boss, is a Sherpa, too. If you have a large group, you may have a few other Sherpas along who look after the front, middle, and particularly the end of the line. If you're in a large group with a couple of Sherpa guides, don't get in front of the first one or behind the last one. It's their job to see that no one gets lost, and there's no reason to make their job harder. If you want to take a break and are behind the others in your group, one of the Sherpas will stay back and wait for you.

   Generally, the *sirdars* and Sherpas carry only their own possessions and the group's medical kit. In a large group, have the Sherpa at the back carry the kit, so it will always be moving toward an injured person.

Cook: The cook is an important member of your team. Like cooks everywhere, he is a high status individual and is treated with utmost respect. Your health depends on him. He will oversee all meal preparations and direct the activities of the "kitchen boys" in hauling water and chopping and stirring food. Like the *sirdar*, the cook will carry only his personal possessions.

Kitchen boys: This job is a porter position with extra prestige. The kitchen boys carry all the kitchen equipment, plus their own possessions, and sometimes food. They will also act as your waiters and generally attend to your needs.

   The *sirdar*, Sherpa, cook, and kitchen boys comprise your basic staff, and you are responsible for supplying all their food. You are also responsible for checking that they have the appropriate clothing if you plan to trek into cold and snow.

Porters: These people do it all! Your *sirdar* will be responsible for the hiring and discharging of the porters as the days go by and the loads lighten. He will determine how many porters you need and what they will carry. To the Westerner, all the loads look too heavy, but there are guidelines and even laws regulating the size and weight of acceptable loads. The *sirdar* knows the rules, so don't question his judgement in these matters.

Porters' wages vary depending on whether you are supplying their food. In general, you won't see much of your porters, since their walking pace and schedule will often be different from yours. At the end of the day, after the loads have been delivered to the campsite, porters tend to disappear into card playing, *bidi* smoking, *rakshi* drinking, singing, and sleeping.

Porters may be men or women, boys or girls, relatively young or old. Many porters may not be familiar with—nor have the necessary clothing/equipment for—higher altitudes, and you may be expected to supply the proper gear. Porters, for the most part, do not carry loads as their sole source of income—many are farmers earning extra money between harvests. If it becomes extremely cold, or if one of the porters is improperly dressed, they'll expect you to lend them some of your extras for temporary use, like traveling over a high, snow-bound pass. To avoid misunderstandings, be sure to distinguish clearly between loans and gifts. Most porters prefer to walk in open, rubber sandals, even in the snow. How they do it is just another one of the mysteries of the high Himalayas.

Your porters will carry their usual 30 kg. (65 lbs.) loads in baskets on their backs, suspended from a "tumpline" strap across their foreheads. They prefer this method to the shoulder straps and hip belts of the scientifically-designed backpack. Loose articles and foodstuffs are put into a *dokols*, these traditional conical bamboo baskets for transporting anything and everything along the trail. (Before paper money was invented, financial transactions were made in coin, and the money was carried in *dokols*.)

At first glance, these baskets don't appear durable, but even if they do break (which is rare), they can be repaired or replaced easily along the way. Lining the basket with plastic sheeting (available in Kathmandu) will keep the

A *traditionally-dressed porter.*

load dry and discourage smaller items from dropping along the trail.

Items carried by porters do receive rough handling, so carry fragile items yourself.

Most of your Nepali crew will not speak English, but they will enjoy learning from you and teaching you some Nepali. You will be strangers at first, but living together on the trail can become a pleasant "family" experience, and you may develop real friendships.

Despite language barriers, you can learn a lot from your crew, just by watching them maneuver on the trail. Take note of their walking style, how they use their knees, and even their pace. For example, they will always pass animals on the uphill side of the trail, because it's easy for a skittish animal to knock someone off the trail altogether.

All transportation costs at the beginning and end of the trek are your responsibility. If you discharge your porters at a site distant from their homes or point of hire, you must pay for their time to return home at half the daily rate. Since the porters won't be carrying a load on their return, the return trip takes less time. Be sure to agree in advance on an estimated number of days of required service.

If a member of your crew becomes sick or injured, you must see that he receives medical attention.

No matter how much staff you decide you need, ask around for the daily rates of pay. If you are going in a reasonably large group (more than six people) for a reasonably long trek (two weeks or more), it's wise to check with the agencies. They have the experience, and you have the confidence of knowing that you will be well cared for.

Small groups with plenty of time to get organized can frequently "do it yourself." If you're going on an independent trek, it's not difficult to hire a porter or two right at the roadhead or landing strip (depending on where you're going), but the reliability and general trekking knowledge of these people may be questionable. Always, however, take someone along.

Cultural Sensitivity

We cannot possibly outline all you could want or need to know about the culture of Nepal. In fact, this lovely little country has so many diverse cultural groups and traditions that anthropologists are still studying them. Many books are available for those people seeking scholarly information, and we recommend that you read as much as you can beforehand (see *Further Reading*).

We will attempt to give you an overview of the customs and habits that you'll most likely encounter along the way. One of the special pleasures of trekking in Nepal is that no matter where you go, you will meet Nepalis going about their lives in traditional ways. Therefore, it's important that you know something about these people and that you respect their culture. The more you know, the easier this can be.

Nepalis are accepting of the cultural transgressions of foreigners, but they are also very appreciative of attempts toward understanding and respect. They will not tell you that you have made a *faux-pas*—after all, you are a guest—but when a succession of gaffes occur, they assume that it's natural for foreigners to be rude and insensitive. Even the most Westernized English-, French-, German-, and even Japanese-speaking Nepalis have their own culture, as well as a set of expectations about yours.

At the risk of great oversimplification, there are two general guidelines to help you in all situations:

The first is simple: be observant and take your cues from the behavior of those around you.

The second is more difficult for Westerners: slow down.

We are constantly in a hurry and tend to get right to the point. This is not the Nepali way. For Nepalis, interpersonal relations, rapport, and respect are more important than the business at hand. Always take things slowly, calmly, and in a friendly manner. Even major disagreements must be handled this way. It can be tough, but if you remember to watch the interactions around you and practice slowing down a little, you'll get along better with your hosts, and you'll enjoy yourself more. After all, you're on vacation!

We could not even begin to write *The Book of Nepali Etiquette*, but we will mention the most common practices and the highest priority do's and don'ts for visitors. Should our tips not cover your needs, it's perfectly acceptable to ask. Nepalis will appreciate your interest.

Religious Sites

In Nepal, most Hindu and Buddhist temples and shrines do not post signs instructing you in the appropriate behavior. However, you will almost always find people performing their ritual observances. Just watch for a while. Don't be too eager to follow along and do what you've just seen. In general, you are a "barbarian" and are excluded from certain sections of the temples and from specific religious practices. The worshippers will probably just ignore you, unless they feel that your behavior is extremely offensive.

Along the trails, you'll find all sorts of sacred places, often easily recognizable by their large size and the artifacts around them. Hindu temples are generally buildings with statuary located nearby, while sacred Buddhist places have a *stupa*, surrounded by cloth prayer flags or carved *mani* stone walls.

These places are not hard to find or identify, but you'll also come upon small, equally sacred places, which you could overlook and accidentally desecrate. Sometimes, the shrine might be just a rock covered with red powder or a small pile of stones. The best thing to do is just leave them alone and, if you have to pass them, go on their left, in a clockwise direction.

> WE REQUEST THAT TO ENTER TH
> TEMPLE OF MUKTINAT WITH SHOES &
> SNAPPING IDOLS OF GOD AND GODESS
> IS EXTREMELY PROHIBITED.
>
> —TOURISM MINISTRY.

Reminder at the Temple of Muktinath.

Signs of Respect

From the moment you arrive, you'll see people greeting one another with "*namaste*." The word is accompanied with a gesture of putting the palms of the hands together with the finger tips about chin-height, while giving a slight nod of the head. Used as a general greeting and also as a gesture of good-bye, it's always appropriate and is far more common than a Western handshake. The word *namaste* is difficult to translate, but it connotes an attitude of respect for the other person's soul and is said with warmth to friends and strangers.

As in many cultures, elderly people in Nepal represent family heritage and wisdom. Although the elderly continue to work very hard, they are always treated with the utmost respect. It's a nice gesture to ask for permission to take their photograph. Don't be insulted if a young Nepali refers to you as mother/father (*amah/baa*), or even grandmother/grandfather (*bajha/bhajha*), although older sister/brother (*didi/dhai*) is more common. They may even ask your age so they can show the proper respect.

In Kathmandu, you can buy a little Nepali-English dictionary, which gives fascinating hints to the culture. Nepalis always appreciate an attempt to speak a bit of the language. They'll treat even your worst fumbling with good humor.

In the major cities, you'll meet Westernized Nepalis, and you can learn a lot about Nepali culture from them. Don't be surprised if they can't answer all your questions. We tend to ask for complete explanations of customs and rituals that most people do not know much about, beyond "that's just the way it is." They're not trying to hide anything; they just don't know, and they often find our curiosity fascinating, although a bit bizarre.

Once trekking, you'll have many chances to meet the traditional village Nepalis. Village children, going to and from school, love to practice their English. Don't be surprised if they ask strange, personal questions, like my favorite: "And what is the occupation of your uncle?" Often, their questions are part of a textbook dialogue. Retired Gurkha soldiers also love to use their English. You can depend on them for a delightful and informative conversation. In any case, the general guidelines apply: take it slow, watch, and if possible, ask.

Eating in a Nepali Home

Whether you are tenting or teashopping, you may be invited into someone's home. Sharing a simple meal in a family setting can be a marvelous experience. It can also be a bit intimidating, since you'll be nervous about doing the right thing. Here are a few pointers:

Before entering the house, take off your shoes. You may see a pile of assorted footwear nearby, but if not, leave your shoes just outside the doorway. It is okay to keep your socks on.

Once inside, greet each person with a *namaste*, beginning with the eldest. Each person will reply in turn, but it could be that not everyone in the room is a family member and may not be actively involved with you, the guest. After the greetings, you should tell them your name, if they don't already know it. Most likely, you won't be addressed by name, and you may never be told all of their names, but it will help you feel more comfortable if you have introduced yourself.

You will be directed to a place to sit, probably on the floor near the fireplace. Though Westerners quickly tire of sitting on the floor and begin squirming about, it's very important that you never end up in a position with the soles of your feet pointing at anyone, or with your legs outstretched so someone could be forced to step over you. Both are serious taboos and are related to the belief that the bottoms of feet are extremely impure—a notion you can probably accept if you think about some of the things you walked through on the trail.

You must also avoid stepping over anyone else. Just wait a fraction of a second, and the obstructing person will get out of your way. It's not seen as an inconvenience, just good manners.

Next, your hosts will offer tea, or possibly homemade alcohol, while you are waiting for the meal to be prepared. All of these activities may be centered around the hearth, which may be the only source of light and heat. Most Westerners view a fire as a convenient place to discard old supermarket receipts, gum wrappers, or traffic citations. You'll be tempted to burn the used tissues and scraps of paper you've stored in your pockets all day. Don't do it! A Nepali cooking fire is sacred. Such trash will contaminate it, delay your dinner, and probably shorten your visit. After all the meal preparations and eating are finished, then you can burn your rubbish. In doubt? Ask.

When the meal is ready, you'll likely be the first one served, and your hostess will give you the normal portion of rice—about twice the amount you could possibly eat. If this happens, it's timely and courteous to ask for a smaller portion, before you even think of tasting it. You'll be offered seconds regardless, but it's most discourteous to waste food.

No one shares his food, and, except for infants, no one eats off another's plate. If you are given a spoon or fork, never put it into a cooking or serving pot, or take food (even leftovers) from someone else. Don't even offer your leftovers to someone else. Only the food on your plate is for you to eat. If you would like more, just wait and it will be offered. Keep in mind, however, that the food you see may well be all there is for the entire family.

Since most Nepalis eat with their hands, there may not be any utensils for you. They assume that you washed your hands before you came, so be sure to do so. Whether you've been given a spoon or are eating with your fingers, do not use your left hand. An explanation of this taboo is in the section on "toileting."

When the meal is finished, your host will pass a container of water around. This is for rinsing your right hand, and you do this directly over your dinner plate. The meal is now over. You'll be invited to sit around and visit, and perhaps enjoy some local whiskey, but it's probably quite late. If you do stay for a while—which is fine—you'll notice that most of the family will ignore you and just go about their business, getting ready for bed. Often, the men will stay up late drinking, and it is okay to join them. Just remember that tomorrow you'll probably be getting up early and walking most of the day.

The family won't expect any sort of gift. You will know from the start whether you've been invited as the family's guest or as a paying customer. Both are possible, but the former would be the result of a relatively lengthy interaction with a family member outside the home. Of course, you can always donate a little something, but if you are a guest, don't offer money.

Should you become lost or severely off schedule, you may need to ask a Nepali if you can eat in his home and possibly spend the night. In this case, you can donate whatever food you have, and you'll be billed for a total amount when you leave. Don't expect any deductions for what you contributed, and don't be totally put-off if your request is denied. It could be that the family does not have any surplus food on hand, or that they are very high-caste and cannot accommodate you. It is okay to ask at any home for a cup of tea and pay the going rate.

Local customs and family practices vary from place to place, as in your own country. So keep your eyes open, relax, and ask. Whatever experiences you have, you're unlikely to be bored or disappointed.

Postcards Home: A Two Week Trek Diary

Day 1: Arrived in Kathmandu intact. The city bustles with expectations—Nepal's and my own. This place is medieval (almost): art, architecture, and ritual practice everywhere, even beside the local pizza parlor. Trekking arrangements proceed. Two more days to shed an ever-so-slight high altitude/jet lag headache and get my legs in the mood . . .

Day 2: Went by Chinese tramline to old Bhaktapur, a wonderfully restored and protected walled city. Peaceful ride through the countryside. Bhaktapur is a pleasant change from the confusion of Kathmandu. There's a timeless quality to the place despite hawkers, beggars, and tourists with wide-angle lenses. The Newars were (are!) exquisite craftsmen in wood, stone, and metal work. Must return to B'pur after trek.

Day 3: Final check of gear and provisions. Everything piled up would rival the height of a lesser Himalayan peak! How much peanut butter will 8 people eat in 8 days? Looks good for early AM departure. Wandered the Asantole bazaar for last minute essentials: safety pins, spare boot laces, and 6 more rolls of film. Nepal eats film. With a little restraint, a roll a day should do it.

Day 4: Land Rover arrived at 6:00am. Long, windy trip west, above river gorges, thru small villages. Too many overland trucks and overloaded buses barrell-

ing down the center of the two lane road for a relaxing nap. Himalayas make a high horizon. Hillsides terraced to the top, stacking 18 million people into this
tiny country. Great Nepali lunch in Mugling—like a
roadside rest stop during the Crusades. Walked only
an hour and a half uphill to first night's campsite.
Peace and quiet (?) with smiling children begging for
candy, "one rupee," and "Are you having a pen for
me?" Clear skies . . . I'm ready for anything.

Day 5: Woke to "bed-tea" and sunshine. Watched
porters arrange and hoist loads. Incredible. My own
pack seemed puny— 'til the serious trekking began.
Glad we have these extra folks along. 3 hour morning
walk thru the middle hills. Low altitude sweat repaid
with views of green valleys and much village activity.
A blessed 2 hour lunch (rest, not food). More walking, then camped in an after-hours schoolyard. Too
tired to write more, and this was only a two blister
"easy day."

Day 6: Colder AM. Legs not bad but shoulders ache.
Pre-trek training should have included climbing all
those stairs with a full pack. Walked through *forests* of
wild orchids until lunch. First view of snow mountains: closer, awesome, and more to come. Nepali
crew is terrific—good food and plenty of it. Lots of
laughter. So very, very happy to be here! Wish you
were, too.

Day 7: Fewer villages, more private campsite. Getting
the knack of personal hygiene—all flows normally
thus far. Having mastered the rhythm of our days, my
mind wanders freely on the trail, unaware of the long
hours of leg-work. The thin air is exhilarating. Natural
beauty everywhere, and a crisp silence that relaxes
the soul. Sleeping well, despite the cold. Last night,
wore all my layers and had a shot of brandy as well.
Water bottle froze in the tent. So many stars . . .

Day 8: Crossed our first precarious suspension
bridge, a bouncing and swaying relic above a roaring
river. It beats 2 extra hours down and another 3 up,

Above Naudanda, a place to catch your breath and enjoy the view.

though, and it's a real tribute to the Ingenuity of Man. Couldn't that herd of goats have waited 'til I crossed, with my feet firmly planted on the other side?! Peaks all around in the distance; wild flowers under foot. Spectacular dawns and sunsets. Hallelujah!

Day 9: Snow shower and a slippery trail. First injury: twisted knee, nothing serious. Thank Brahma, Vishnu, and the porter who carried me, the trek goes on. Great timing: tomorrow is REST DAY. Saw village wedding in progress. Wonderful hospitality with drums, horns, and singing. Wish I'd brought a tape recorder. Beautiful people. Magnificent jewelry!!!

Day 10: Morning wash-up (first full body wash and full load of laundry) at village well. Short walk (up) to ancient shrine for lunch. Time for reading, writing, sunning the old bones, and delightful non-commun-ication with a weaving grandmother. Bought her woolen sash hot off the loom. This place is too beautiful to leave. Yet, already, tomorrow we start our return.

Day 11: More oxygen, more warmth. Downhill harder on the knees. Lots of stone walls and houses now. Fields of millet and mangy dogs. Fewer porters with us, as we eat our way thru the supplies. Fresh apples for sale in the village—like meeting an old friend in an unexpected place! Love the simplicity of the trekker's life. No modern conveniences to reckon with. Took my watch off one nameless day last week. Any wars been declared lately?

Day 12: Final 7 hours of walking. A day of mourning—the end of an affair? I'll miss the golden glow of my nylon roof in AM sun, the mountains of starch called "mealtime," the solitary space of being so far away from everything familiar. I see colors I never knew existed, hear sounds with the clarity of a concert master. My body is a precision machine, my mind is blissfully uncluttered. This is more than a holiday . . .

Day 13: Back in Kathmandu. Traffic noises, crowds, solid walls and floors. Also hot water, clean clothes, new food selections, a haircut, and a vigorous massage. My pack lies limply in the corner of my room, my film lines up like soldiers on the dresser. Can photos take me back to the high mountains? Must once-in-a-lifetime experiences come only once? Now, off to the bazaar again, for gifts and mementos to try to make all this magic real. Two weeks was not enough . . .

An Introduction to Healthy Trekking

One of the primary purposes of this book is to put the common medical concerns about trekking in Nepal into proper perspective. Most people worry about their health while traveling in Asia, and such concern is realistic. Chances are, you will become at least mildly sick at some point during your trip. But you don't have to assume the worst, and the more knowledge you have about what is "lying in wait" for you, the better your chances of minimizing the negative effects.

We're making the following health and first aid recommendations in the interest of healthy and enjoyable trekking. We are not medical practitioners and cannot make any pronouncements on how to deal with fractures, internal injuries, or other serious medical problems. People with chronic health problems should consult a physician before they commit to any trek. Though health posts are scattered about the hills, they are inadequately equipped (by Western standards) and sporadically staffed—totally unsuitable for any major medical emergency.

We have included the medications mentioned in this section (and in the *Medical Kit Supply List* which follows) because they work and are available in Kathmandu without prescription. But availability varies, as does "medication of choice." We urge you to check with your doctor before you leave. He/she may have alternative suggestions.

Other than hospitals in Kathmandu and Pokhara, the only reasonable medical facilities are the two Himalayan

Rescue Association facilities on the Annapurna circuit and at Pheriche in the Solu-Khumbu region. A United Mission Hospital is located outside of Gorkha, and a British Hospital is in Dharan in the eastern Terai. No matter where you are when you encounter major medical difficulties, you could face a two or three day walk to one of these facilities. And house calls are rare! Though you can send a runner to the nearest health post, there's no guarantee that anyone will be there who can help you.

Therefore, if you or someone in your group is having major medical troubles along the trek, you have only one option: *get out of the mountains.* You can hire yaks, ponies, or porters to transport injured people to the nearest hospital or roadhead. In general, planes to Kathmandu will give priority to the seriously ill. Further, District Centers and some police check posts maintain shortwave radios to send messages for helicopter rescue. Specific instructions for this are described in the section on helicopter rescue.

Medically, you are pretty much on your own while trekking. The route you choose and the commitment you make should be directly related to your physical and mental preparedness.

Caring for Other Trekkers

You must also be prepared to extend this commitment to the people who accompany you. We've heard shocking and sad stories about sick or injured trekkers who were abandoned by their companions and left to fend for themselves—occasionally with fatal outcomes.

When you team up with others, you should automatically accept responsibility for each other. While this is not an issue for people trekking with an agency-hired staff, it is a frequent problem for small groups of independent trekkers. No sick or injured person should ever be left alone. It's far wiser for everyone to use healthy common sense and to look after one another along the way.

Once you assume this sort of responsibility, trekking can get a bit tricky. Sick people often will try to minimize their troubles so as not to burden the group. At the other extreme, a weak trekker may make an undue commotion about a relatively minor ailment. These kinds of dilemmas result in people being left behind!

Since each occurrence will be unique, we can't tell you the "right way" to deal with this issue. We can only advise you to be honest, responsible, and not in too much of a hurry.

Common Medical Concerns

Our advice is intended to cover the most frequent, and generally minor, medical difficulties. We're assuming that all trekkers want to stay as healthy as possible. A cavalier attitude toward your health risks serious and painful problems and can jeopardize your entire trek. Be sensible, ask a lot of questions before you leave, and most of all, be realistic about the type of commitment you are making.

The following sections of first aid common sense are organized somewhat like a trek: we start in the lowest region, your feet, and travel to the highest area, your head. In trekking, this is a rather obvious route, but as a format for medical information, it may be a bit confusing. We've tried to keep things logical, so just keep making your way through these sections, in the same way you'll be making your way along the trail. In both cases, we hope that you'll emerge somewhere at the other end, healthy, happy, and confident.

Blisters: Just about all trekkers have some problem with their feet. Well-fitting boots and a supply of clean, holeless socks provide the best prevention. Even so, you're likely to get blisters, which can be very painful and annoying.

Blister remedies are available in outdoor supply shops in the West, and new ones appear all the time. In Nepal, the most common solution is *moleskin*, a heavy, flannel adhesive patch which can be cut to the appropriate size. Unfortunately, the only moleskin carried by the trekking supply shops in Nepal is the surplus that trekkers leave behind, so its availability is sporadic. Bring your own moleskin or a similar product, and be on the lookout for it while you are cruising the shops for other equipment.

The best way to deal with blisters is to have the strength of character to avoid getting them. While this may sound a bit farfetched, it's really true. As you start out each morning in your clean socks and comfortable shoes, you'll be just getting into the rhythm of walking when you may feel a bit of heat somewhere on a foot. In another hour, this hot spot will be a blister. It takes strength of character to acknowledge the problem—after all, you've been walking only 20 minutes—and have the discipline to treat it immediately. If you can avoid blisters in the first few days, you'll probably avoid them altogether.

The technique for treatment is simple, once you decide to sit down and do it. Remove your shoe and find the offending area: it will probably be red and tender to the touch. Simply cut a patch of moleskin to cover the hot spot, peel off the back, and stick it on. That's it. Leave the patch on and let it absorb the abrasions. Eventually it will fall off; taking it off risks removing the top layer of skin you're trying to protect.

If you didn't manage to get to it while it was a small hot spot, you might have a real blister to deal with. This may be a bit trickier, but it's not an overwhelming medical maneuver. Again, cut a patch to cover the area, and you may decide that it warrants two layers.

If you've really been appreciating the view and disregarding the distress signals from your feet, you may have a lovely "mushroom cloud" blister. If so, you can get quite creative with moleskin. The best way is to cut a doughnut to go around the blister and then, with the appropriate number of layers, build up, doughnut upon doughnut, until you can cover the blister with a final, solid patch. It can be bulky and uncomfortable, but it's far better than popping the blister, which leaves your foot vulnerable to infection.

Other tips: Take off your boots at rest stops to air your feet and dry out your socks. Washing your feet and your socks frequently also helps, but wearing wet socks is not a good idea. Cutting your toenails and keeping them trimmed may make your boots more comfortable. Adjust the tightness of the laces, particularly the lower section over your arch to keep your foot from sliding forward on the long downhills. Alternating between pairs of shoes evens out the wear on your feet.

Frostbite: Frostbite is much harder to get than blisters, and you'll have to pay more attention to the symptoms. The best prevention, again, is appropriate clothing and equipment. Insulating socks and sturdy boots are best, as well as insulating gloves/mittens and something to cover your ears. Your feet are the most vulnerable to frostbite, because they carry you through the snow and get cold and wet. If it was difficult to stop and deal with a hot spot, it's even harder to stop when your feet are freezing.

The first signs of frostbite are redness and tingling, followed by numbness and gradual color changes from bluish to white. Frostbite can be very serious and can ruin

your feet and your trip. When your feet begin to feel very cold, make an effort to warm them as soon as possible. Remove your boots and socks, and get your feet dry. Then get them into a sleeping bag or next to someone else's stomach (a true of test friendship). Do **not** put them near a fire or into hot water. Your feet must warm up gradually, and harsh treatment can damage the tissues.

Frostbite comes in degrees, like burns, and can be extremely painful. The best prevention is proper footwear for cold and snow and an awareness of the condition of your feet. Keep an eye on your companions as well, and see that your Nepali team is adequately shod.

Leeches: Another problem associated with feet—although not limited to them—is leeches. Check yourself, particularly the warm, moist places, from time to time for leeches. These creatures respect no privacy.

Although this topic is somewhat repulsive, there are a few bright spots. First, leeches are seasonal, and they tend to find you only in the warmer, lower elevations during and after the rainy season. They make great stories ("You should have seen the one that got away!"), and while they are disgusting, they are quite small and not too serious. Your first leech is the worst.

Probably you'll discover a small, bloody patch on your

sock, or someone else will notice fresh blood trickling down your leg. Congratulations, you've been leeched—and you never even saw the sucker. Leech bites are not painful and rarely get infected. The creature secretes a blood anticoagulant, which causes about 20 minutes of bleeding after it drank its fill quickly and moved on. Basically, they create a laundry problem (dried blood stains are tough).

If you are unfortunate enough to catch a leech in action, you have a number of choices. The scientific types can calmly observe their specimen, while the rest of us let out a wild scream and try to get rid of it. You can pour a bit of iodine on it, sprinkle it with salt, or use the native technique: Nepalis usually just grimace, pull the critter off, and throw it away.

The Nepali leech does not leave its head behind or anything else for that matter, except a small, bloody hole. Consider them only a grim reminder that you are far away from home, and be happy if you have a Band-Aid nearby.

Joint and Muscle Strains: Ankles and knees can take a beating while trekking. Many people suffer some joint discomfort on the trail, caused by hours of walking, the weight of a pack, and the diverse terrain. Even the flattest path is likely to be strewn with rocks or loose dirt that can twist an ankle or cause a wrenching fall. Plus, going uphill uses one set of muscles; coming down uses another. Many trekkers don't even realize they *have* some of these muscles until they discover how sore they are.

You can take a few, sensible precautions. First, have appropriate footwear and concentrate on the trail. Watching for birds as you walk is not a good idea. When you really want to look at something, stop and enjoy it. You can even sit down and give yourself a little rest!

Bring a few Ace bandages, the elastic wrap kind that come in a variety of widths. The three-inch width—the most functional—is available in Kathmandu. The Indian-made bandages lose their elasticity quickly, so Western ones are better and can be used over and over. Mostly, Ace bandages provide extra support to a tired, strained, or sprained ankle or knee. Of course, people with chronic muscle or joint problems should come with a more

substantial brace or other device recommended by a doctor.

A painful, swollen, but not serious, condition known as "Sahib's Knee" usually occurs after a long, downhill stretch. Two aspirin and an Ace bandage will add a measure of comfort, inhibit additional swelling, and give a boost to morale. Be sure you don't wrap the bandage too tightly, and check to see that your extremities are not changing color due to poor circulation.

After a few days, ankles and knees generally strengthen, but if you continue to have problems, consider getting a walking stick. You can often buy nicely carved sticks, sometimes from their makers, along the trail. Otherwise, wooded areas provide free models that you can tailor to your specifications. A sturdy walking stick adds stability and can become a faithful companion. If you decide to carry a stick, beware of getting yet another blister—this time on your thumb.

Snake and Animal Bites: There are many varieties of snakes in Nepal, and some of them are poisonous, but most snakes do not like the cold of the higher elevations. In fact, it's rare for trekkers to even see a snake, and it's even rarer for a trekker to be bitten.

However, snakes are out there, so be reasonably cautious. They will be as fearful of you as you are of them, but if you are venturing into tall grass or thick brush for privacy, it's a good idea to rattle around a bit before you assume a posture that might inhibit a quick getaway.

If a snake bites you—and remember, this is *very* unlikely—remain calm. Getting excited only increases the speed at which the venom will travel through your bloodstream. First, try to determine if the snake is poisonous by looking at the wound. Non-poisonous snakes usually have rows of teeth and tend to tear a chunk of flesh when they bite. However, if there are two distinct punctures, the snake was probably poisonous.

Since you can't plan on the kind of snake that's waiting to bite you, you can't bring antivenin. (Anyway, antivenin is best administered by a doctor.) The more information you can get about the snake—color, length, distinguishing features, habitat, etc.—the easier identification will be. If you really think the snake was poisonous, get out of the mountains as soon as possible. No matter what, stay calm and treat the wound as you would any animal bite.

Rabies does exist in Nepal, and trekkers should use common sense in dealing with any wild animal. Remember, the lick of a rabid dog on an open hangnail can be as serious as a bite.

If an animal bites someone, keep calm, wash the wound with soap for 20 minutes under running water, and make it bleed. Then clean it with disinfectant and cover it as needed. Try to observe the behavior of the animal, but not all rabid animals foam at the mouth, and few wild animals wait around while you watch them.

The treatment for rabies today is not as severe as it used to be, but the only sure way to know if an animal is infected is by a laboratory analysis of the animal's brain. It's far easier to use extreme caution around all animals. Be prepared to head back immediately if you are bitten. You have ten days before rabies shots should begin.

It is possible to get an immunization against rabies. The vaccine is safe, effective, and inexpensive, compared to the lengthy treatment necessary if you get bit by a rabid animal. But animal and snake bites should be easy to avoid. Just use common sense.

Abrasions, Contusions, and Other Petty Annoyances: Along with blisters, minor cuts and scrapes are the most common ailments of trekkers. Treat cuts and scrapes first with soap and water, then clean with an antiseptic, and, if possible, leave the wound open to promote rapid healing.

If the wound needs to be covered, clean it with a drying antiseptic like Betadine, or even Lugol's iodine. Try to avoid antiseptic creams, since they keep the skin damp, thereby increasing the risk of infection. Soap and water, disinfectant, and Band-Aids usually work just fine.

Minor burns may require an antibiotic cream. If the burned skin is blistered or broken, cover it loosely. Apply something cold immediately to reduce the pain of a burn. For severe burns, seek medical attention as quickly as possible.

For bigger cuts—the kind that gape open and might need a few stitches—*butterfly bandages* work well and are often used now instead of a needle and thread. Apply pressure directly on the wound to stop bleeding, then clean it (as outlined above for small cuts). You can buy butterfly bandages, or you make your own easily from ordinary adhesive tape:

Cut a piece of tape the appropriate length for good adhesion *across* the line of the wound—an inch or so (2-3cm) for a finger, perhaps three inches (8cm) for an arm or leg wound. Narrow tape, not much wider than an half-inch or so works best, so you may want to cut wider tape lengthwise as well. Use scissors to make four diagonal incisions toward the center of the strip (see diagram).

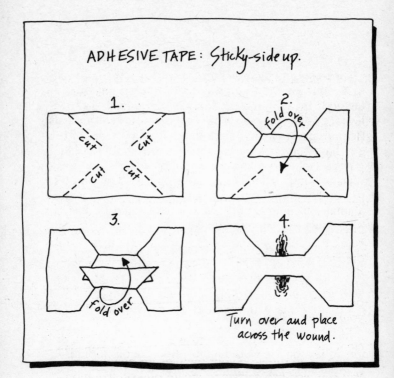

ADHESIVE TAPE: Sticky-side up.

1. *cut* *cut* *cut* *cut*

2. fold over

3. fold over

4. Turn over and place across the wound.

Then carefully fold the free flaps over one another to seal off the adhesive. It is this thin central strip that will be directly above—perpendicular to, but not stuck to—the cut.

If the cut is long, use more than one butterfly spaced out along the full length. After you have cleaned and disinfected the cut, let the skin around it dry before you try to stick on the butterflies. First, attach one side of the butterfly to the skin and gently pull the bandage across the wound, bringing the edges of the cut together. Secure them by fastening the other end of the butterfly bandage to the skin on the other side. Then you just cover the cut as needed, right over the butterflies. Change the covering dressing periodically to keep the area clean, but don't remove the original butterflies until the edges of the cut begin to knit together firmly.

If you've made these little fellas carefully, they won't be stuck on the cut itself, and they'll allow air to circulate freely under the strips. It's a good idea to practice on a minor cut, so if you do encounter a first class butterfly situation, you'll feel like you know what you're doing.

For excessive bleeding, try to elevate the wound away from the heart and use continued pressure on the cut itself. Tourniquets have gone out of style. Unless you really know what you're doing with a tourniquet, you risk endangering an entire limb. Use pressure—sanitary napkins are great for big cuts—and then make some monster butterflies. Always beware of infection.

Insect bites, stinging nettles, and bee stings are also common complaints. Though small animals like puppies and goats look cuddly, most have ticks and fleas, so avoid picking them up. If you are staying in teashops, check to see if there is anything crawling around before you lay out your sleeping bag. A plastic sheet between you and the mattress may keep you happier during the night. Bring some insect repellent to use as needed. A few drops on a neckerchief will keep annoying swarms away from your head.

Buy a small tin of Tiger Balm in Kathmandu. This ancient herbal medicine is great for superficial skin itches, and you can rub it on your temples for headaches, too. You can also use cortisone cream on skin irritations. If you really want to go native, Nepalis often smear the itchy, stinging area with mucus.

Allergic reactions can occur, so bring a mild antihistamine, like Actifed, Incidil, or slightly stronger Benadryl. Be careful, however, as Benadryl (50 mg every 4-6 hours) is highly sedative. It's best taken only at bedtime. If you do have an allergic reaction—inordinate swelling, redness, hives, or difficulty breathing—to an insect bite or medication, drink extra fluids, preferably water, and stop using that medication.

Strains, Sprains, and Fractures: Trekkers often experience a minor fall that results in the painful swelling of a joint. A leg injury can create difficulties, since the victim must continue walking or be carried. Arm problems are somewhat easier to handle, but in either case, the victim should rest frequently and be relieved of his pack. It's also a nice gesture to relieve the injured person of any guilt he may be carrying about delaying others in the group. An injury is everyone's business.

Strains: A strain is just the miserable ache of over-use.

88

It will go away with rest, reassurance, and aspirin.

Sprains, involving muscles, tendons, or ligaments, are often not so cooperative or quick to heal. To treat a sprain, make the victim comfortable and keep him warm, elevate the injured limb, assess for possible fracture, apply cold compresses to reduce the pain and swelling, wrap the injured joint with Ace bandages for support (and to minimize swelling), give aspirin for pain, advise rest and immobility, and wait 24 hours to see how it develops.

For severe pain, two aspirin every four hours should be fine, or take the aspirin in combination with codeine (60 mg. every four hours). But use codeine with caution, since it's an opiate-based drug, and many people are allergic to it. Should nausea, vomiting, or other discomforts arise, discontinue its use.

Only an x-ray can verify a **fracture**, but there are a few things to look for if you suspect a broken bone. First, see if the limb is disfigured. That is, aside from swelling, is it the same shape as—and symmetrical to—the other limb? If not, it's probably a break, and a doctor should treat it as soon as possible. Do what you can to devise a splint, immobilize the limb, and make the injured person as comfortable as possible, with as little movement as possible. You must get the victim out of the mountains.

Legs in General: The first few days or so can be a bit uncomfortable as your body does its best to protest the unusual activity. Don't be fooled into thinking that you have discovered all the potential aches after the first long day of uphill walking. If it's any consolation, what went up must come down. The muscles that worked so faithfully to get you up will now get a bit of a rest, and a whole new set of muscles will take over to get you down again. If you're really hurting and it feels like some trekking demon has replaced your legs with two aching logs, take 2 or 5 mg. of Valium, a muscle relaxant, when you're ready to retire (expire?) for the night.

Crotch Rot and Chafing: It's not uncommon for men and women to develop an annoying chafing in the upper thigh area, or for men to get a case of crotch rot. The best prevention is to keep clean and wear loose, soft, and com-

Take Ibuprofin + aspirin

fortable clothes. Lotions and baby powder can be soothing, but the circulation of air whenever possible will clear up the problem best.

Stomach and Lower G.I. Problems: The best way to keep your stomach and bowels functioning well is to use your head.

The traveler's fear of diarrhea—usually out of proportion to the actual suffering involved—tends to diminish with experience. Of course, trekkers should try to maintain the best hygiene they can, but conditions aren't always accommodating. You should assume that your tummy won't be normal, at least some of the time.

Do not be misled into thinking that a drop of rainwater is a deadly agent of disease, or that you can develop immunity to the local "beasties." Drink only treated, bottled, or boiled water, and drink a lot of it (four to five liters per day) while trekking.

One happy note: You cannot become infected by bathing (or even washing your cuts) in untreated water. However, you should brush your teeth only with treated water.

If you're trekking with an agency, your Nepali crew will prepare water properly and fill your canteen in the morning. It's a wonderful service, but one canteen is usually not enough to satisfy your body's water needs. Though some trekkers rely on sodas or beer if available along the route, such liquids aren't really what your body needs, either. Even the hot, sweet, milky Nepali tea, which is quite safe to drink, is not as effective as plain water, properly treated.

Water Treatment and Purification: This is the big one! The best method to purify water is to boil and filter it thoroughly. Though there is some debate over how long to boil water and at what point the offending organisms get killed, this is not really your problem. Even if you are told that the water has been thoroughly boiled, remain skeptical and develop a taste for (or at least a tolerance of) iodine-flavored water. After that, everything gets relatively easy.

To purify a standard canteen (quart/liter size), add six to ten drops of Lugol's liquid iodine or 2% Tincture of

Iodine, depending on how dirty the water looks. Though you can't see the critters swimming in your canteen, you can bet that the more cloudy the water, the more contaminated it is. Water temperature also determines how effective the treatment will be. Generally, the colder the water, the longer and more intense the treatment dosage should be.

To keep it as simple as possible, we always use eight drops of iodine (which we carry in a small, squeezeable bottle—found easily at home but with great difficulty in Kathmandu) and wait 20 to 30 minutes before drinking. With iodine tablets, we use one per quart/liter, and we wait 20 to 30 minutes after the tablet dissolves completely.

Some people are allergic to iodine, and other methods of chemical purification are available—consult your trekking supply shop. Also, new portable filters claim to purify water that's simply poured through them. While we have witnessed a filter turn Kool-Aid into plain water, we have not seen it remove bacteria, viruses, or parasites. As of this writing, these filters have not been field tested in Nepal.

The water you'll be drinking can come from just about anywhere: rivers, lakes, wells, and "let's not inquire." Considering the population density and poor sanitation of Nepal, it's safe to assume that *all* water is contaminated, though this probably is not the case, especially at the higher elevations.

But leave the debate to the bacteriologists. Drink only properly treated water, and learn to purify it yourself to ensure that it's done properly. You can't drink too much water on your trek, and what you drink must be treated. Sip your way through the day, and take a long drink before you refill your canteen and treat the new water. That way, a half hour can elapse without your gasping while you watch the clock.

Basically, water purification is just another little habit you need to develop as part of your trekking lifestyle. Do the best you can, and don't be surprised if you develop a little tummy trouble along the way. This, too, is part of the experience.

Diarrhea: There are three main causes of trekker's diarrhea, but with any diarrhea you should wait at least 24 hours before beginning a drug treatment, during which time you should drink lots of fluids and eat moderately.

Bacterial diarrhea, the most common, usually begins abruptly with frequent watery stools accompanied by cramping and perhaps fever. Bacterial diarrhea often goes away on its own. But if symptoms are severe, treatment will shorten the length of the illness.
Treatment: Bactrim DS, one tablet every 12 hours for three days (people allergic to sulfa drugs should avoid this) or nalidixic acid, 500 mg., two tablets every six hours for three days (not for children under 18). If you want the most complete treatment possible, take the full dose of nalidixic acid along with 250 mg. of erythromycin every six hours for three days. This covers almost all the bacterial possibilities.

Giardia is a protozoan which causes low-grade diarrhea, gas, and tiredness. There is almost never any fever associated with giardia, but a lot of sulfuric burps and gas are common.
Treatment: Tinidazole (Tiniba), 500 mg. Take four tablets (two grams) all at once, one time. Tiniba causes a metallic taste in the mouth and occasional nausea. It cannot be taken with alcohol.

Amoebic diarrhea is characterized by chronic, frequent small stools, painful cramping, and persistent, vague pain. Weight loss is common after a few weeks.
Treatment: Tinidazole (Tiniba), 500 mg. Take four tablets (two grams) all at once for three days. Then take 500 mg. of dilxanide furoate (Furamide) three times a day for ten days. Do not take the Tiniba with alcohol.

Remember, don't begin medicating your diarrhea too quickly. Often it will go away by itself. If you don't know which type you have, you may be taking the wrong medicine altogether.
It's not uncommon for people to have a combination of causes, so get a doctor's diagnosis if your diarrhea is really stubborn. Even if you've taken medication, have a stool sample tested before you leave Nepal. Tests can

be done at the Central Clinic, New Road; Kalimati Clinic, Kalimati; or Ciwec Clinic, across from the Russian Embassy. To have similar tests performed back home and medication prescribed can be a lengthy and expensive proposition.

Warning about Lomotil: Lomotil is a very strong drug which will stop diarrhea—dead! It works its magic by completely incapacitating the intestine. It is not recommended for use while trekking, where toilet facilities are as close as the nearest bush. However, you might want to take some along if you'll be returning to Kathmandu via a long bus ride. Use Lomotil only with utmost caution.

Rather than trying to stop up your diarrhea, you are better off trying to flush it out. Drink as much as you can, including light soups. Yogurt and plain rice are good for additional nutrition.

Sometimes, people develop such severe intestinal problems that they vomit and have diarrhea simultaneously. Obviously, they are very ill and probably would benefit from oral rehydration salts (Jeevan Jel). Such salts—unnecessary for normal cases of diarrhea—should be reserved for people who can't keep food down at all.

All diarrheas are caused by ingesting contaminated food or water. While most places that serve visitors try to follow hygienic procedures, obviously a lot of errors are made. All you can do is control what you eat and avoid the most likely contaminants. No matter how careful you are, you're still a candidate for illness, so select your eating places with care and try to eat only freshly cooked foods. In public places and private homes, the dishwater is never treated. If possible, see that your plate, drinking glass, and utensils are thoroughly dry before your food is served. Do what you can to be vigilant, then relax and enjoy your meals.

Constipation: After all this talk about diarrhea, you might not believe that constipation could even exist. It does, and it's a common complaint among trekkers, especially women.

There are two main causes of constipation in trekkers, and both are easy to remedy. The first is a failure to drink enough fluids. On a trek, your body will require far more

Rural health post at Tukche during rush hour.

fluid than normal to maintain proper hydration. If you are uncomfortably constipated, you'll need to drink more water—even if you feel you're going to explode. It's better to take frequent, small drinks rather than try to finish off an entire canteen at once. Keep your water bottle handy—don't bury it in your pack—and sip your way along.

Constipation's other cause is usually the absence of pastel bathroom tiles, color coordinated toilet tissues, Sani-Flush deodorizer, and a locking door. Well, what can we say? Eventually, you'll get used to it, though you'll probably never really enjoy it. Take your time, relax, and, if necessary, take some laxative.

Worms: Another routine precaution—done every six months or so by Nepal residents—is deworming. Intestinal worms are a common, though mild, complaint, especially among children, who tend to eat without washing their hands. The incubation time for worms can be lengthy, and you may not know immediately that you have them.

In Nepal, Mebex or Wormin are broad spectrum deworming medicines with simple directions. Worm medicine in the U.S. can be expensive unless prescribed by a veterinarian, so it's a good idea to wash your hands frequently in Nepal—and take along a souvenir packet of Mebex or Wormin when you leave.

Backs and Shoulders: Severe back injuries and the care of chronic back problems are beyond the scope of this book. Nevertheless, normal backs and shoulders are prone to strain and fatigue from carrying heavy loads and walking long distances.

The best cure is a little prevention: carry a properly packed backpack of appropriate size and weight for you. If the straps of your pack cause chafing across your collar bones, place two adhesive-backed sanitary napkins on your shoulders to provide an extra layer of padding. They will relieve the pain until your skin toughens up.

Another good cure for sore backs: liniment (or massage oil) and a willing companion. Also, check your route for hot springs, scattered throughout Nepal. While the facilities are never five-star-spa style, the hot water does wonders on the aches, pains, and general grime of a trail-weary trekker. If you're not lucky enough to come upon one of these impromptu resorts, the only other advice we can give is to take two aspirin and call us in the morning.

A frequent, though minor, complaint of trekkers is a slight swelling of hands and fingers. Don't be alarmed— altitude and exertion are usually the culprits, and the swelling will subside as your body adjusts to the trek.

Head: The most common problems associated with the head are headaches and sunburn, but trekkers also complain of coughing, eye strain, and even toothaches.

Headaches: Most people develop a headache at some point, and the causes are many. Just take two aspirin. The most serious headache, a symptom of altitude sickness, will not respond to aspirin. We will discuss this life-threatening condition below.

Sunburn: Sunburn complaints range from minor irritants to major problems, especially at higher altitudes where the air is thin. Wear a hat and use lotion or sunblock as needed. Don't forget the back of your neck and your ears. If you are wearing shorts (men only, please), be sure to protect your thighs and the backs of your knees. When adjusting your body temperature by removing layers, try not to remove your hat as the heat increases. The sun can be very strong even if the air is cool, and, if it's reflected off snow, it can be quite dangerous.

Eye Problems: To protect against snow blindness, we recommend glacier glasses, the ones with very dark lenses and side-flaps. You can rent them in Kathmandu. If you expect to spend a good bit of time in snow country, bring a few extra pairs for your guides. Even regular sunglasses are better than nothing.

If you wear prescription glasses, it's a very good idea to bring an extra pair. Glasses do get stepped on, and we even heard of a pair that leapt into a river, leaving the owner angry and nearsighted. Contact lens wearers report no special problems, other than dust. They recommend the usual care routines, as well as bringing a pair of regular specs. Sterilized water can be scarce, so bring plenty of soaking solution.

Conjunctivitis (pink eye) is common, especially during the dusty winter months. Pink eye is extremely contagious and requires a lot of handwashing to inhibit its spread. The first signs are bloodshot eyes, soreness, and that gummy, stuck-shut feeling in your eyes when you wake up. If not treated, conjunctivitis can become serious and painful. Use sulfacetamide 10% drops—one drop, four times a day, for three to five days. Wash your hands immediately after treatment. If conjunctivitis develops in one eye, you should treat the other eye, too: it's only a matter of time before it spreads.

Breathing Problems: There's nothing worse on a trek than having a cough, or sharing a tent with someone who does. Benadryl is quite good for a nagging nighttime cough. For a really severe cough, however, codeine in very small doses at night will act as a suppressant. During the day, lozenges are fine.

At night, **Cheyne-Stokes Breathing**, a fairly common difficulty, can occur at the higher altitudes. Cheyne-Stokes involves a pattern of irregular breathing while you sleep, causing you to wake up gasping for air, afraid that you cannot breathe at all! Though it can be very distressing to you and the people around you, it's not a symptom of anything serious. It indicates only that you are working harder to get a normal amount of oxygen into your lungs, and it may make you extremely tired the next day. Usually, the condition lasts only a few nights.

Dental Care: There are no dentists in the foothills and mountains of Nepal. In fact, fewer than 30 dentists serve the entire country of eighteen million people. If you develop a toothache, you're on your own. Fillings can fall out, and unfortunately, the rice sometimes has small rocks in it which can break a tooth. Packing a hurt tooth with cotton-wool soaked in oil of cloves is an excellent interim measure. Take aspirin for pain.

If things get really tough, ask the villagers for their home remedies. Most of them have never seen a dentist and never will, but they undoubtedly get toothaches, and they just might have a pair of pliers. (Most Nepalis believe that worms cause tooth decay.)

You will meet many darling children along the way who will ask you for candy (*mithai*). Give them raisins or cookies instead—it's better for their teeth, and it's just as generous. It's hard for Westerners to believe, but people in Nepal die from poor oral hygiene, and toothbrushes are almost as rare as dentists.

Lice: While walking through villages, you will see quaint scenes of entire families sitting in sunny doorways, delousing. Though this makes a great photograph, lice are unpleasant companions on your trek.

If you are staying in teashops, you need to take extra precautions against lice. Use your groundsheet under your sleeping bag, and be sure to use something that's your own as a pillow. You can also get lice by trying on hats and patting little children on the head. (By the way, it is extremely impolite to touch any Nepali on the head, though the taboo is not related to lice. If you pat them, pat their shoulder instead.)

The best cure for lice is Licel, available in Kathmandu chemist shops. It's easy to use.

Malaria: Caused by the bite of a particular mosquito, malaria is most prevalent in the Terai, Nepal's lowland jungle region in the south. Most people living in Kathmandu do not routinely use malaria suppressants and do not take them for trekking.

If you will be in the lowlands, possibly rafting or visiting one of the jungle lodges, you should begin prophylactic treatment for malaria one week before possible exposure. Most people use chloroquine phosphate. Dosage is 500 mg. for adults. For children, dosages vary depending on the child's weight. Generally, you take one dose the week before going to the Terai.

The most important suppressant therapy is not the dose taken in the area, but the weekly dose you take for six weeks *after* leaving. It's essential that you take the weekly dose, so set a particular time on a particular day to do this.

AMS, Acclimatization, and Helicopter Rescue

The following chapter is perhaps the most important in the book. It could save your life! The Himalayan Rescue Association (HRA), a non-profit organization which strives to reduce casualties in the Nepal Himalayas, provided this information.

The HRA, founded in 1973, operates rescue posts along the two most popular trekking routes: one in Pheriche on the way to Mt. Everest, the other in Manang, just before the Thorang Pass on the Annapurna circuit. Both posts are staffed by volunteer doctors during the main trekking seasons.

The HRA operates solely on donations. In Kathmandu, their office is located in front of the Kathmandu Guest House in Thamel, just around the corner from many trekking supply shops. We urge everyone to stop there for additional trekking information (and to make a small donation).

AMS

One of the most serious medical problems you can encounter on a trek is **Acute Mountain Sickness** (AMS). You can develop AMS at any altitude over 6,500 feet (1,975 meters), but it's most common when you are sleeping above 12,000 feet (3,650 meters). AMS is the result of fluid accumulating in either the brain, the lungs, or both. Fortunately, it can be avoided.

The best prevention is called *acclimatization*—that is, giving your body adequate time to adjust to the increased altitude. Being in a hurry in the mountains can be dead-ly! Prepare your schedule so you ascend no more than 1,300 feet (395 meters) per day when you're above 10,000 feet (3,040 meters).

If you fail to allow time for acclimatization, you may develop symptoms of AMS. If you ignore them, you're asking for serious trouble. The initial symptoms of AMS—headache, fatigue, loss of appetite, breathlessness (even while resting)—may be mild and should vanish with a day's rest at the same altitude. Just stay put and enjoy your locale an extra day before going farther and higher.

When mild symptoms occur, stay at your current altitude until they go away. Never ascend with any symptoms of AMS, except for a really quick trip over a pass, which would allow a rapid, immediate descent on other side. AMS does not allow you much leisure time, other than just staying put until the earliest symptoms disappear.

If you are resting at the same altitude and the symptoms get worse, then you must descend immediately. Worsening symptoms include increasing tiredness, severe headache, vomiting, coughing, and loss of coordination. If ignored, these symptoms could spark fatal complications.

A person suffering from AMS may not be thinking clearly, so you might have to force him to descend. Even if the victim is willing to descend, never let him go alone. If the victim can't walk, get a yak, pony, or even a porter to carry him. Do not delay the descent, and continue heading down until the victim shows some signs of improvement. This usually happens after 1,000-1,500 feet (300-450 meters). Even if the diagnosis of AMS is uncertain, de-scend. You can always climb back later when the person is feeling better.

In sum: If you aren't feeling well at high altitudes, you probably have some mild symptoms of AMS. Rest at the same altitude until you feel well. If you get worse at the same altitude, descend to at least the last point at which you felt well. If you're not sure of the diagnosis, always err on the side of being too cautious.

A Few More Points on AMS

• Physical fitness does not prevent AMS. Going slowly does.

• The HRA does not recommend taking any drugs to try to prevent AMS. Just ascend slowly.

• If you are pregnant or have heart disease, do not go above 12,000 feet (3,650 meters).

• Not everyone in your group will acclimate at the same rate. Be prepared to rest when needed, or split the group if necessary. But never leave anyone behind, alone.

• Infants who can't tell you how they feel should not be taken to high altitudes, and watch young children closely.

• Don't take sleeping pills and other sedatives at high altitudes, since they tend to decrease breathing and may lead to AMS.

• Above 12,000 feet (3,650 meters), sleep at the same altitude for two nights.

• Then, do not set up camp more than 1,500 feet (450 meters) higher than your previous camp.

• If you have flown to a site above 12,000 feet (3,650 meters), take the extra precaution of two rest days before proceeding.

• No special precautions are required on descent.

Helicopter Rescue

The Royal Nepalese Army Wing Command will provide evacuation by helicopter for severely injured or ill trekkers. However, someone in Kathmandu must guarantee payment for the flight *before* the rescue. Rescue missions cost $600 (U.S.) per flying hour, and the average rescue flight costs $1,200-$2,000.

If you are trekking with a Kathmandu-based agency, send the rescue request to them, and they will arrange the flight. If you are trekking on your own, send the message to your embassy. They will need your name, nationality, location, and the details of the injury or sickness.

You can transmit messages through the police radio system, the National Park radio system, or the local airports. It almost always takes at least 24 hours to arrange a rescue, including the time for relaying the message.

If your home country has an embassy in Kathmandu, register with them before your trek and record the details of rescue insurance, if you have it. This will speed up the rescue process. If your country does not have an embassy or consulate in Kathmandu, and if you're trekking on your own, you will have trouble getting rescued unless you made arrangements in advance. One possibility is to leave money with a trekking agency before you go.

If you do call for a rescue, be sure to give a detailed description of your location, and then make it identifiable from the air. Placing bright colored clothes at a suitable landing spot will be helpful to the pilot. Then, stay put until the helicopter comes.

If you see a helicopter circling overhead as though it's trying to locate someone, do not wave your arms unless you are the person who called for the rescue. Doing so risks an unnecessary landing, which will delay the actual rescue effort and jeopardize the safety of the helicopter crew.

Trekkers' Medical Kit

The following list of medicines and first aid preparations is by no means all-inclusive. Rather, we created it to inform you of those items you are most likely to need. All items are listed as 1st, 2nd, or 3rd priority needs. Of course, you should modify this list depending on your known needs, destination, size of your group, and length of your trek.

If you are trekking with an agency, they will supply a substantial medical kit, but it's still a good idea to read through this material, just for the sake of familiarity.

The quantities given are suitable for a 14-day trek by a group of 12.

Priority	Item/Quantity	What For?	How to Use/Dosage
1	moleskin, molefoam, etc. (1 pkg)	blisters, hot spots	Cut to appropriate size, and apply to spot immediately
1	Ace bandages (3-4 wraps)	sprains, strains	Wrap firmly (but not tight) around the ailing joint for additional support. Check extremities for reduced circulation.

1	Lugol's Liquid Iodine (1-2 bottles)/iodine tablets	water purification (liquid can be used as antiseptic and to remove leeches or ticks)	(Check instructions) Liquid: eight drops per liter, wait 20 minutes. Tablets: one per liter, wait 20 minutes
1	Tylenol (regular strength) (1 bottle)	Fever, pain	Children under 100 lbs: 1 tablet every 3-4 hours, as needed (2 tablets may be given to children for severe pain). Children and adults over 100 lbs: 2 tablets every 3-4 hours, as needed
1	Tiniba (12 tablets)	Most commonly used drug on trek. For diarrhea	For giardia: 2 grams once For amoebas: 2 grams daily for 3 days
1	aspirin (1 bottle)	For muscle and joint pain, it's better than Tylenol, since it is an anti-inflammatory and reduces swelling	Same as Tylenol

Priority	Item/Quantity	What For?	How to Use/Dosage
1	amoxicillin (40 tablets)	antibiotic for ear infections, bronchitis, general antibiotic needs	250mg four times a day for 10 days **NOTE:** You must take this drug for 10 days **CAUTION:** This is a penicillin drug and can cause allergic reactions.
1	cephalexin (Sporadex) (40 tablets)	antibiotic for skin infections	250 mg four times a day for 10 days
1	erythromycin (40 tablets)	antibiotic for people allergic to penicillin	250 mg four times a day for 7-10 days
1	Benadryl (1 bottle)	allergic reactions to plants, insects, drugs	Adults: 50 mg every 4-6 hours as needed Children: 25 mg every 4-6 hours as needed. It's best used at night. **NOTE:** Benadryl is highly sedative. For allergic reactions to penicillin: force fluids and give 25 or 50 mg of Benadryl. (50 mg to a child under 100 lbs. may cause him to sleep over 12 hours.)
1	Betadine (1 bottle)	skin antiseptic: use after soap and water on cuts and scrapes	Do not pour Betadine directly into a deep wound: apply to a bandage instead.

1	gauze (6-8 squares, 3 rolls)	for covering large wounds, or can be cut to size bandages
1	Band-Aids (1 box)	as needed to keep small wounds clean and allow air to circulate
1	sunscreen/sunblock (1 bottle)	as needed for protection, particularly nose and back of neck and knees
1	cotton wool swabs (moderate quantity)	extremely useful for cleaning wounds and applying antiseptic
1	scissors/Swiss Army knife	for all cutting needs: adhesive tape, moleskin, fingernails and toenails, etc.
1	tweezers	to remove splinters, etc.
2	codeine (6 tablets)	for severe pain, or severe cough at night — with aspirin for severe joint or muscle pain: 15 mg every four hours for children; 60 mg every four hours for adults. **NOTE:** Codeine is an opiate and may cause allergic reactions. Use without aspirin for other severe pain.

Priority	Item/Quantity	What For?	How to Use/Dosage
2	thermometer	to take temperature	as needed
2	sulfacetamide 10% drops	for severe eye irritations, or conjunctivitis (pink eye)	1 drop four times a day for 3-5 days
2	Jeevan Jel oral salts (6 packets)	for rehydration, especially with vomiting and diarrhea	follow directions on packet
2	cortisone cream/ Tiger Balm	for plant rashes, hives, insect bites, etc.	apply as needed to control itching
2	Actifed/Incidil (12 tablets)	antihistamine for cold symptoms, mild allergic reactions	1 tablet as needed
2	insect repellant	mosquitoes, etc.	as needed
2	cough suppressant/ decongestant/lozenges	coughs, sore throat, etc.	as needed

3	Valium (10 tablets)	muscle relaxant for soreness so extreme that it may prevent sleep	1 tablet (5 mg) at bedtime, but do not take above 10,000 feet (3,000 meters)
3	Lomotil	to stop diarrhea	**Beware:** Use only on long bus/plane rides
3	oil of cloves	for toothache pain	paint onto tooth as needed
3	laxative	for constipation	follow directions, as needed.

The Five Minute Medical Kit

Now that you've got all this stuff and know how to use it, how are you going to carry it? It's a lot of medicine and it's not exactly light, but you want it to be readily accessible.

If you have a Nepali team, give the kit to the guide who will be staying at the end of the line. He won't even notice the extra weight, and the kit will always be handy (or at least not far behind you). Do not give the kit to a porter, who will make it disappear into a well-packed *dokol*. You may not be able to locate either the kit or the porter when you need them quickly.

If you trek without a porter or guide, then you'll be carrying it. Be sure not to stuff it so deep in your pack that you need hours to retrieve it.

Either way, we suggest you create a **Five Minute Medical Kit**, which will contain the most likely needed items in a given five minute span. Make one of these for each member of your group, since it's annoying when you must rummage through the "central store" for a small piece of moleskin or an aspirin.

Your Five Minute Kit should include: (carry myself)

- Band-Aids (medium sized)
- small bottle of disinfectant
- moleskin, molefoam, etc.
- iodine for water purification
- aspirin or Tylenol
- insect repellant
- Tiger Balm

- assorted bits of gauze, tape, cotton, Q-tips
- Swiss Army knife or scissors
- Ace bandage
- sunscreen
- lozenges

A small plastic bag keeps everything dry, if not particularly tidy. Usually, you'll have every medical item you'll need right with you, and you can resupply as needed at mealtimes. It's a good idea to keep a small bar of soap handy as well, for personal hygiene and first aid.

Medical Treatment of Nepalis Along the Way

As you travel through villages, Nepalis will assume that you are carrying medical supplies and that someone in your group is a doctor. You'll probably have more medicine on hand than most rural health posts, and the combined knowledge of first aid in your group probably will be substantial. So don't be surprised when you are asked to observe, consult, and treat a range of medical problems.

If you have no medical training, here lies a dilemma, and there are a variety of opinions on this matter. We will outline briefly some of the sentiments, but ultimately, the choice is yours.

Some Western medical people believe that when Nepalis ask your medical advice or request medicine, you should do nothing but encourage them to go to the nearest medical outpost or hospital. They maintain that you'll probably misdiagnose the ailment, you could actually mask a more serious problem that requires professional treatment. They also feel that dispensing antibiotics is a mistake. Nepalis don't understand Western medical principles, and they probably won't take the medication properly. (After all, we all know well-educated people who stop taking their medicine once they start to feel better.) Further, giving Nepalis drugs will increase their resistance to the drugs, possibly prompting more severe problems in the future.

An opposing opinion says that you should do whatever you can and hope for the best. After all, you may encounter some desperate illnesses, and it's only natural to want to help however you can.

Of course, you and your group could later need the medicine you're giving away, but that isn't really the issue. The point is that you will be moving on, often in a few minutes, and you'll never know the result of your "treatment." So, unless you *are* a doctor, to act like one is probably more foolish than helpful. Nepal is not the place to indulge your Schweitzerian fantasies.

Soap and Water

From our experience, we advise the soap-and-water course of treatment. Most of the minor problems you'll encounter result from bad hygiene: infected cuts, scrapes, and insect bites which would not have become so badly infected if they had been cleaned properly. Unfortunately, soap wasn't available when the injury occurred, and yours might be the only bar around.

We make it a habit to collect "donations" of small bars of soap from hotels and airlines throughout the year, in preparation for trekking. We distribute them as needed, and we always give a good, frothy demonstration of their use. Remember, what you do has a major educational impact, so do it up big, with lots of suds and water. (We sometimes add a splash of disinfectant and an oversized bandage, too.) For our finale, we give a lengthy discourse on the continued use of the soap, and we recommend that it be saved for future accidents.

You may be asked for antibiotics, but we don't give out anything stronger than aspirin, and then only if the circumstances warrant it.

Always urge people to go to the health posts. Granted, the posts are few and far between, but the health system will never get more government funds if it is underutilized. Also, at the last health post we pass, we try to leave behind appropriate, unused medical supplies from our kit. They may be only a drop in the bucket, but the donation satisfies our desire to help.

While the "nothing stronger than soap, water, and aspirin" approach may seem a bit callous, we've found it to be a workable compromise in a very difficult situation. Of course, if you are on the scene when a serious accident occurs, you should do all you can to help.

Chances are, you'll be treating a member of your Nepali team for some health problem at some point along the trek. In this event, you can be a little more "doctorish," since you'll be on hand to see that he continues his treatment properly.

Trekking
with Children

Children differ in age, physical ability, and adaptability to strange environments, so advice on trekking with kids can never get too specific. However, in our years of trekking with dozens of children, ages 3-18, we've learned a a few things worth sharing.

In general, trekking with children is a great experience. A small child's perceptions can add magic to your hike: a boring stretch of woods might become Hansel and Gretel's forest to a child. Plus, Nepalis love children, and a child may open doors that otherwise would remain closed.

If you can, bring more than one child on the trek. Children tend to get bored looking at scenery, and a companion to explore a village or skip rocks in a river can make the trek more fun, thereby increasing their willingness to proceed. An exhausted, stubborn child can destroy your tranquility.

If you are planning to take children, we strongly recommend that you trek with an agency—and with tents. Many agencies have long experience in family trekking, and sleeping in tents gives kids an additional element of adventure. Also, tents provide a flexibility that can be useful in adjusting the length of your trekking days to a child's needs. Campsite activity always fascinates children, and most of them will form warm relationships with your Nepali team. A child will walk far longer and more happily with a laughing *sirdar* than with Mom and Dad.

Physical Concerns

Most children over age eight can manage six hours of walking without difficulty. They can be slow, particularly in the afternoon, but they can also be surprisingly fast, leaving you far behind. A child's walking pace tends to be very irregular: fast, slow, "I can't take another step," then racing on ahead. Fortunately, this works itself out after a few days when they get accustomed to the rhythm of the trek.

Of course, children should never walk completely alone, but it's fine to let them get a little bit ahead and feel as though they are explorers. Also, of course, never let a child be the last one in the group. Always station an adult at the end of the line.

It can be difficult—and frankly, annoying—to have to constantly adjust your pace to that of a pokey child. Kids tend to want to rest "just for a minute" at the bottom of a big hill—just when you feel that if you sit down, you'll never get up again. So if you have a younger child along, consider hiring an extra porter who can carry the child if necessary. Many women porters, easily hired through any agency, love to do this. The child may not want or need to be carried all the time, but a porter provides a nice alternative to stopping or having to carry the kid yourself!

An extra porter is a fairly inexpensive luxury—one that you'll really appreciate if you get to the top of a hill, sit down to enjoy the view, and watch your child and his companion porter come up the trail to join you. Sometimes, of course, it's the other way around—they'll be watching you!

Equipment and Health

The equipment and health care advice that applies to adults also applies to kids. But be sure to monitor a child's fluid intake, since they will forget to drink enough or say they aren't thirsty. A little sweet flavoring for their water will mask the taste of the iodine. Frequent, short water breaks and a handful of raisins or nuts will keep a child moving along (adults, too, for that matter).

Children can be fussy about strange foods, or even familiar foods prepared differently, so pack some familiar goodies (not necessarily candy) to appease them. Even the pickiest eaters eventually get too hungry and will eat what's offered. Most children will eat soup without complaint, and it's a good way to add liquid to their diet.

While some children react negatively to the filth they see around them, others enthusiastically ''go native.'' Regardless of your feelings on the subject, kids **must** wash their hands thoroughly before eating, and make sure they observe the requirements of properly treated drinking water. You'll be amazed at how quickly they accept these rules as part of the game.

Trekking with Infants

Trekking with infants is possible, but in the interest of safety, you'll need to plan a fairly unambitious outing. Again, we recommend you go with an agency.

Infants may be more prone to altitude sickness than children, since their temperature-regulating mechanisms work differently. Since they can't really tell you how they feel, you should be very careful. But trekking is not impossible with an infant. A short trek in the middle hills (from 4,000-8,000 feet) can be very enjoyable and offers great scenery without the temperature extremes of higher altitudes.

A few years ago, a friend came to Nepal with a 10-month old, and we took a trek through the middle hills and had a terrific time. She had a baby-backpack device, carried by a porter, and she discovered that walking slightly behind the porter allowed the baby to focus elsewhere and also gave her a feeling of independence (though she was still close by). A water bottle, pacifier, hat, and even shoes were tied to the carrier frame and allowed to dangle, so they wouldn't be constantly dropped onto the ground. And the infant could choose when to use the bottle and pacifier. This—and disposable diapers, properly disposed of—made the trip work surprisingly well.

Perhaps the most wonderful thing about trekking with children is to watch their transformation. Children return from a trek with a remarkable sense of independence and self-confidence. Best of all, the effects stay with them. Even the most materialistic, self-absorbed teenagers return with a new outlook on their relative affluence. They appreciate the beauty of the countryside, but they also always empathize with their porter, poorly clothed, possibly barefoot, working very hard for very little money—and he may not be any older than they are. If for no other reason, bring the children along. It's well worth the investment.

Medical Kit for Kids

The basic supplies you already have in your medical kit are correct for children as well, though there is some concern about giving aspirin to children. If you're bringing the kids, it's a good idea to have the following:

• Tylenol or other non-aspirin analgesic for routine needs. While aspirin is better for muscle pain, Tylenol is better at high altitudes and when there is nausea.

• Dramamine is useful for motion sickness in buses or airplanes. It has no other uses on a trek. Interestingly, swallowing a piece of fresh ginger has the same effect.

• Pepto-Bismol is a great thing to have for children. Its pink color and sweet taste does a lot for stomach upsets, and it's helpful for diarrhea.

A Bit
About the Terai

Bordering on India, the Terai is the southernmost region of Nepal. Since it is flat and relatively hot year-round (50° [10°C] in winter to above 100° [38°C] during the monsoon months), it is not a popular trekking area. We'd like to discuss it briefly, however, because many people visit the Terai, and it has myriad attractions.

This lowland area of Nepal is the nation's breadbasket and has three annual growing cycles. There is fertile soil and abundant water flowing from the northern mountains. Recently, foreign aid projects have created irrigation systems, and since the near-eradication of malaria, the Government has been encouraging migration from the overcrowded hill areas.

Unfortunately, this increased population pressure has disrupted the natural jungle ecosystem and the economy of the indigenous Tharu people. The statuesque Tharus are primarily farmers and are easily identifiable by their relative tallness, darker complexions, and the elaborate tattoos on the backs of the women. Little is known about their origins, but they have lived in the Terai for centuries and have a natural immunity to malaria.

Primarily, the Terai is the place to see abundant wildlife. The 360 square miles (932 square kilometers) of **Royal Chitwan National Park** is the primary wildlife preserve, located 75 miles (120 kilometers) from Kathmandu and a short distance south of the major east-west highway. It can be reached by road, air, or raft. There are a number of smaller wildlife preserves in the Terai as well, but these are more remote and difficult to visit. (All national parks

117

in Nepal require Visitor Permits, purchased at the park's entrance offices.)

For lodging, the top-of-the-line jungle lodge is **Tiger Tops**, although there are other good choices—**Gaida Wildlife Camp**, **Hotel Elephant Camp**, and **Jungle Safari Camp**—which vary in prices and services. In general, they range from $50-$100 per day. All have offices in Kathmandu and, as part of the package, will arrange transportation to the Park, as well as safaris by foot, boat, Land Rover, or elephant into the jungle. Any Kathmandu trekking agency can direct you to these offices, and the larger agencies can make the necessary arrangements.

The best time to visit the Terai is between October and April, between monsoons, although by April it can be extremely hot. Once there, you can expect to see the one-horned rhinoceros, many species of monkeys and deer, large and small jungle cats (including possibly a Bengal tiger), and much more. The park also has over 300 species of birds and 100 species of butterflies and moths. During the winter months, you get spectacular views of the Himalayan peaks far to the north.

While the accommodations within the park and on its immediate perimeter tend to be expensive, the budget traveler does not have to forgo a visit. Buses from Kathmandu will take you to Narayanghat, where you can arrange for local transport to Tadi Bazaar and then south to the park entrance in the village of Saurah. There are teashop-type hotels in Saurah, and guides can be hired for visits into the park.

Like trekking, it's better not to go into the park alone. Chitwan is not a zoo with wildlife securely behind bars and popcorn stands every hundred yards. It's also advisable to take malaria suppressants before you get there.

After a long and strenuous trekking adventure, many people like to conclude their visit to Nepal with a few days of more passive activity in the Terai. It's definitely a treat and certainly worth a visit.

Rafting in Nepal: A New Adventure

For a fascinating contrast of experiences within a single holiday, many people enjoy a leisurely raft trip after a strenuous trek.

Rafting on the rivers of Nepal is an increasingly popular tourist activity, and for good reason. A rafting trip takes you down magnificent river gorges, through exciting rapids, and along quiet, lazy stretches where you can watch birds and riverside village activities. Plus, you don't even need river-running experience.

Rafting trips do require planning. Unlike trekking, there is no way you can do it independently. You must hire a rafting outfitter who will, if nothing else, supply the raft. You can make arrangements in advance through **Force 10 Expeditions** and **Himalayan Travels**. Both offer rafting trips on the Trisuli River down to Chitwan National Park. Many agencies in Kathmandu offer similar raft trips/park visit combinations.

Longer river trips generally use the Sunkhosi River in eastern Nepal. **Wilderness Travel**, for example, has a 10-day package on the Sunkhosi, and **Above the Clouds Trekking** offers a river trip that emphasizes the cultural aspects of Nepal.

You can always make arrangements in Kathmandu with outfitters like **Summit Hotel Trekking** or **Himalayan River Expeditions**. Prices vary greatly, depending on the length of the trip, transportation arrangements, and type of service. In general, a rafting trip involves road transportation from Kathmandu to your put-in site, lunch for a one-day trip or complete provisions (including tents) for a long

Kali Gandaki Gorge.

trip, and then return transportation when it's over. Prices begin at $25 per day.

Things to Consider

Before committing to a raft trip, you need to consider a number of things, because once you're on the river there's no way to turn around and go back.

First consideration is the season of the year. Although the weather in Nepal is not totally predictable, the rivers are full and powerful during the summer monsoon, and a raft trip can be a thrilling ride. The water is lower in the winter and spring months, but that doesn't mean a river trip will be less exciting. In fact, some of the most exhilarating rapids—hardly noticeable when the rivers are fuller—appear in the drier seasons.

The rivers, like the weather, are changeable, and the reliable outfitters know where and when to take you. The most placid stretches of water can hide hazardous eddies, undercurrents, and large boulders. Falling out of a raft may involve more than getting wet. However, the most common complaint is sunburn.

Shop around and ask a lot of questions: What kind of rafts do they use? How many people are in a raft? How are the oarsmen trained? Trained by whom? Do they have river rescue training? Is it a "do-it-yourself" paddling trip? Are waterproof bags, life-jackets, and helmets provided? What are the transportation, food, and tenting arrangements?

Talk to people and get as much information as you can, especially about safety precautions. If possible, interview the actual boatmen, rather than the people in the office. Unfortunately, some of the newer outfitters, trying to get in on a good thing, do not fully appreciate the potential hazards on the river, and an easy place to trim costs is training and safety procedures.

In general, you can assume you'll get exactly the kind of rafting trip you are paying for. *Caveat rafter.*

U.S. *agencies mentioned*:

Force 10 Expeditions
PO Box 547
New Canaan, CT 06840
800-888-9400
203-966-2691

Himalayan Travel
PO Box 481-0
Greenwich, CT 06836
800-225-2380
203-622-6777

Wilderness Travel
1760 Solano Ave.
Berkeley, CA 94707
800-247-6700
415-524-5111

Above the Clouds Trekking
PO Box 398E
Worcester, MA 01602
800-233-4499
508-799-4499

A *rhododendron forest above Chitre.*

Happy Trekking!

You are on your way to a wonderful adventure.

You'll be "walking around" in some of the world's most beautiful hills, surrounded by some of the world's most beautiful people. You will undoubtedly experience other superlatives as well: gorgeous river valleys, exotic animals and flowers, fascinating buildings, the lovely music of birds, the wind, and even the dogs barking on distant hillsides. Perhaps the most breathtaking experience of all is the vast silence, best enjoyed with your camera tucked away and your eyes closed.

Your fingers will find beauty in the textures of the rocks and the mosses. Your aching legs will find beauty in a brief rest on a sunny stone wall. Your nose will savor glorious smells in a damp forest, and your tired feet will tingle after a dunk in a cold stream.

The Nepali people deeply appreciate the beauty around them, though they don't talk about it much. When things go badly, they simply tilt their heads and say "K*e garne*?" ("What to do?").

For a happy trekking experience, try to practice some of this *ke garne* attitude. When things go badly, tilt your head, smile, and then look around at the beauty. It's everywhere. If you take a moment to locate it, observe it, and then appreciate it, your trekking adventure will become far more than just a walk around in the hills. You will discover the deeper richness and beauty of Nepal, and you may discover a richness and beauty within yourself, as well.

Namaste, and happy trekking!

Appendix I:
Tips for the Health Freak

We've created this appendix for people who want to know more about posture and other physical considerations involved in trekking. It's included especially for people with back, knee, or ankle problems, since the unique demands of trekking require more attention and preparation than ordinary walking. We hope this section will give you information that will enhance your trekking pleasure.

"But I'm already in good shape!"

Most people realize they should do some physical conditioning before their trek, but the question of just what to do often stops them from doing anything. With today's popularity for fitness—jogging, aerobics, tennis, etc.—it's easy to think that you're in decent shape and that you really don't need to do anything more. Unfortunately, it's rarely true, and it's often the "fit" people who ignore physical warning signals and get into trouble on the trail.

An experienced squash player is ready for the demands of routine play, but how well will the squash player's body respond to a four hour, uphill walk in 80° heat? Just because you run five miles a day, don't assume that trekking will be a breeze.

Of course, any exercise routine is better than none, but the best form of trek conditioning is trekking itself. This is why professional climbers take two weeks to walk to Everest Base Camp instead of flying there!

Your pre-trek fitness program should emphasize preparation for the unique physical demands of trekking:

pacing considerations, daily warm-up routine, three-day acclimatization routine, breathing awareness, proper walking checklist, and relaxation.

General Pacing Considerations

You will enjoy your trek more if you maintain a flexible trekking itinerary. Give yourself plenty of time to relax and enjoy the pleasant and unplanned events along the way. Your trek will offer unique weather, scenery, wildlife, people, and places, and it's a shame to miss them because of a tight schedule.

Hurriedness creates tension, and stress can become a factor in accidents. Walking after dark, skipping meals, forgetting to drink water, or not getting enough rest—all to meet a wristwatch setting or map destination—do not contribute to a healthy, relaxing, or satisfying holiday.

The most important, time-sensitive aspect of a trek is your body's need to acclimate to the elevation and the new surroundings and equipment. This process affects just about every aspect of your trip, including the food you eat, the pack you carry, the physical activity, the accommodations, and the general "foreignness" of the entire adventure. Your enthusiasm and excitement the first day on the trail may tempt you to do more than you should. So, good planning, especially for the first three days on the trail, can set the tone for a more comfortable, pain-free trek.

The time you spend to break in your equipment and your muscles will pay off later. Pace yourself, and, from the very beginning, take the time to enjoy where you are and what you're doing.

A Daily Warm-up Routine

Use warm-up exercises that gently stretch the muscles of your neck, shoulder, back, legs, and ankles. If you have a regular morning routine, try to follow it on the trek. Be alert to areas of your body that are feeling stress, and give them a little extra attention.

The sooner you develop an exercise routine before you leave for the trek, the better you'll be on the trail.

Stretching, the first element of self-care, is preventive. Simple stretching exercises can do a lot to help you avoid more serious problems later on. Even muscles that are screaming their objections to further use will benefit from a gentle, slow stretch. We recommend the following stretching routine:

• Assume a position that pulls gently on the area you want to stretch.

• Place a little bit more stretch into the position than is comfortable.

• Hold the position and take 10-15 long, deep breaths, increasing the stretch slowly as the muscles relax and feel more comfortable.

• Begin and end your stretches slowly and easily, and be sure to stretch both sides of your body evenly.

NOTE: Never bounce, strain, or force your muscles. Let your breathing stretch and relax you. After all, relaxation is what it's all about.

Three-Day Acclimatization

Day 1: Get up early, pack your gear, treat your water, have a good breakfast, and do a few warm-up exercises and stretches. Check your map and plan a half-day walk. Take your time, rest frequently, drink plenty of water, and get a feel for your equipment and walking rhythm. After three or four hours of serious walking, you've done enough. You should be at a lunch stop and ready to eat, so relax, pat yourself on the back, and take the rest of the day off.

Day 2: When you wake up, your legs will probably be sore from yesterday's hike. This second morning's routine is about the same as the first's, but the exercises are more important—and perhaps a bit more painful. So do those stretches, and try not to skip the ones that hurt the most.

Today you should take a three to four hour morning walk, resting and drinking along the way, and then relax over lunch. Plan to hike another three hours after lunch to your campsite. Try to choose a quiet campsite as a reward for your first full day of trekking.

Day 3: Today you're a real trekker, and you should feel ready for pleasant hours of walking along the trail. Don't forget the exercises even though you feel fit, since the terrain is likely to become steeper and you'll be using a different set of muscles.

The hardest part is gauging how long it will take you to get from Point A to Point B, but by now you should be ready for just about anything. Walking with someone who goes too fast or too slow can be exhausting, so get into your own pace and enjoy the trail. If you're still having difficulties on the third day, acknowledge them and accept that you may need an extra day or two to get yourself synchronized. Keep a positive attitude: it *will* get easier.

Breathing Awareness

Breathing is something most of us don't pay much attention to. In trekking, however, there are advantages to being aware of your rate of respiration.

When you start huffing and puffing, you quickly appreciate the difference between the amount of oxygen you need going uphill and the amount you need going down. Changes in altitude and incline, as well as your level of fitness, will produce changes in your breathing rate. Try to synchronize your breathing with your rate of walking to determine your most comfortable pace.

For example: going uphill, try taking four steps per inhalation and four steps per exhalation. If nothing else, this tends to keep you going at an even pace and gives you something to concentrate on while your heart is pounding in your ears.

The point is, pay some attention to the process of breathing. Controlled breathing can make a difference at the end of a long day, or even at the end of a long ascent. Well-paced trekkers experience fewer injuries and generally feel invigorated rather than exhausted at the end of the day.

The optimal breathing pattern is slow, full, and deep, so both the chest and abdomen expand. Awareness of the depth your breathing and practice will improve your ability to trek at higher altitudes and will help you handle the general stress.

Deep breathing provides an overall feeling of relaxation and well-being, it can help you get a good night's sleep, and it's an excellent way to warm your body. Try it.

A Proper Walking Checklist

• Pack your backpack properly, with the weight evenly distributed.

• Keep your pelvis and hips rolled under to avoid a swayed back.

• Bend your knees slightly.

• Lean forward slightly at the waist when going uphill or carrying a heavy load.

• When you walk, emphasize movement from the knees, rolling on your feet from heel to toe. Don't let your feet pound on the ground.

• Take slow, short steps of as equal lengths as possible. Watch the porters: they "roll" uphill and downhill. On slippery downhills, they tend to go faster rather than slower. They say that they tell themselves they are very light and cannot fall. Though they do fall occasionally, "thinking light" does seem to help.

Relaxation and Self-Care

Almost everyone experiences some kind of tired, sore, aching muscle or joint pain while trekking. After a few days, these complaints usually disappear, but you can do a few things to help the ache. Aspirin will relieve a lot of muscular discomfort, and a good massage helps, too.

For those hard to reach aches, you may need to negotiate with a companion. There's nothing more appreciated on a trek than a friendly massage. An exchange of shoulder rubs can do more to soothe the effects of a hard day than just about anything.

When giving a massage, always direct your movements

toward the heart to improve circulation (e.g., from the hand toward the shoulder, from the foot toward the hip). Use a cream or oil to reduce friction on the skin. If there is swelling, do not massage directly on the swollen area. Instead, massage the area above and below the swelling to increase blood flow and move excess fluid out of the injured area.

When it comes to relaxation, one person's pleasure can be another's irritation. In trekking, you'll usually be dealing with simple problems made worse by fatigue and unfamiliar circumstances. To relax, do whatever works best for you, but since a martini or Beethoven may not be available, you should be open to some alternatives. Try a short nap in the sun, a cup of tea, or just a few minutes alone, enjoying the view.

No matter how smoothly the trek is going or how well you're handling the stresses and strains, you will have moments of pain, frustration, and interpersonal annoyance. But that's just part of the adventure. So relax, accept the difficulties as temporary, and remember the reasons you came to Nepal.

Appendix II:
Why Go Trekking at All?
A True Story

As our small van slid through the mud, twisting and turning in the deep ruts, I reflected on what we were doing, heading east instead of west. Kathmandu was partially flooded and, once again, our long-anticipated and well-planned trek to Annapurna Sanctuary had become impossible.

This time it wasn't because of conflicting work schedules or overcrowded tourist flights to Pokhara—and certainly not because of a lack of resolve. We had tried, really tried, but this time, it was the weather that wouldn't cooperate. The rain, so much for late October, was washing out roads, leaving trekkers stranded on ledges and threatening the country's precarious rice harvest. While the fields were an appropriate lush green, the skies were the ominous grey of the preceding months of monsoon. And now there were thunderstorms and even cyclones blowing in from the Bay of Bengal.

So why were we going trekking at all?

For foreign residents of Nepal, the mountains are constant, though often inaccessible, companions. Trekking seasons conflict with jobs, and when the freedom of a two-week vacation arises, Thailand's beaches and seafood beckon. So Desain, the late autumn Nepali holiday season, offers the time and, in years past, the beautiful views and weather for a trip into the mountains.

This year, the weather was a different story.

We had settled on this trek destination, ostensibly because none of us had been there before. Actually, the sparsely populated and infrequently trekked area of Panch Pokhari, two valleys east of Helambu, offered some planning options: we could make it a five, seven, or nine day trek, depending on weather, leeches, and fortitude.

So there we were, jostling along, occasionally slogging by foot to lighten the van or pushing it to keep moving toward the roadhead at Chautaara. While we kept making cheery comments on how much thinner the clouds looked and how much closer we were to our point of departure, Pasang, my impish friend and knowledgeable Sherpa, kept his eyes on the skies. I tried to coax a smile from him with reminiscences of our previous treks together. Finally, after what for him was a long silence, he gently tilted his head from side to side, Nepali-style, and with a big grin said, "This time, I don't know, Amy Memsahib."

(Actually, Pasang is a Tamang from eastern Nepal, not a Sherpa at all, but every trekker likes to think his guide is "authentic," or better still, a cousin-brother to Tenzing Norkey.)

The drizzle ended and our spirits rose when we reached the final stop, long past any pavement and probably the last place the driver could negotiate a U-turn. Quickly, Pasang found two men willing to work as porters for the extra holiday income. A farmer, Ram, agreed to be our local guide to the five sacred lakes of Panch Pokhari. (Within a few days, however, when we knew him better, we changed his name to Maybe. He was a man of indecisive character, unsure of his authority and our route.)

Our other crew member, Knock-Knee, was a strong, stocky boy of about 15. The silent, stoic type, he rarely spoke to us at all. Each morning he would hoist his 60-pound load of our essentials and then glide effortlessly past us along the trail. Although he was always dressed in overly patched trousers, a grimy, tattered shirt, and the rubber sandals of village attire, somehow he knew all the words to the latest Prince album. He would sing along loudly with a borrowed Walkman on his ears, and he never offered any explanation. Just another Himalayan mystery!

In no time at all we were on the trail, five eager trekkers in search of solitude, scenery, sunshine (we hoped), and not too much adventure. Jim, a Fulbright anthro-pologist, immediately took the lead with the slow, decisive pace of the experienced. He rarely varied his strides, regardless of the angle or terrain.

Right behind him came Adam, our 18-year old athlete, walking with youthful strength and determination despite his heavy pack. Glimpses of Jim's red shirt and Adam's orange pack became frequent trail markers ahead for David, Peter, and me.

We began our ascent with three hours of gentle climbing on a well-worn trail, emerging from the forest onto an alpine meadow. We were all encouraged by the gradually clearing skies and the rolling panorama of green, terraced hillsides. Playful, chanting children greeted us as we walked past their clay-smeared houses, decorated with marigolds for the holidays. All the sights and sounds and smells were welcome intrusions on my lingering thoughts of the unfinished report on my desk and an upcoming schedule of dreary meetings.

The first night, we pitched our tents on a chilly ridge above the last village on the map. Peter, a native of the Canadian Yukon and a recent arrival in Nepal, sat in his shorts watching the glowing sunset. His only remark: "So where's the snow?" The night sky was gloriously clear. In Kathmandu, some stars are always visible, but a short distance from the city, without electric lights and dirty air, the sky becomes congested with pinpoints of light. Only the intermittent bark of a dog interrupted the solitude.

The next morning, we woke to bright sunshine (hooray!) and the clattering of the tea kettle outside our tents. Pasang's greeting, "Good morning, Memsahib. Bed-tea," was the first of a series of rituals which become the morning devotions of a trek. As we fumbled out of our goose down cocoons to steaming cups of hot, sweet, milky tea, we were also greeted by the entire local population of 15—with assorted livestock—who had come to watch the strange behavior of their overnight visitors.

David, however, was distraught. During the night his comfortable air mattress had efficiently carried his body heat into the ground, hatching hundreds of nylon-eating termites. The ravenous bugs had banqueted their way out of the ground and through the floor of his brand new, top-of-the line, all-weather tent. The pattern of holes was similar to the stars in the night sky.

Five leeches, four blisters, and three hours later, we finally came to our first relatively flat stretch after somehow climbing a steep, rock-strewn gully, made slippery by the rain. Now we floated along a gradual incline, surrounded by pine and rhododendron hung with wisps of grey-green moss. Soon we were above the tree line altogether and looking forward to glimpses of the mountain peaks to the north.

Trudging onward, we watched waves of cloud and mist roll up from the valleys to engulf us on the ridge in a cold, sleeting rain. Below and behind, bright pools of elusive sunlight mocked our aching legs and spirits.

The snow underfoot soaked through to David's moleskinned heels and freezing toes. A deskbound doctor trying to satisfy Nepal's desperate need for family planning, he had finally found the time to escape his work and experience this wilderness area. "You know," he said, rubbing his red feet, "in some ways family planning is perfect pre-trek training. No matter how far you get, there's always another obstacle ahead of you."

As we crossed a slushy, scrub-covered meadow, dotted with goat droppings and remnants of herders' encampments, the Himalayan crows jeered our efforts. Just beyond a rock outcropping, we saw our first downhill leg in two long days of climbing. And beyond, far higher than the eye normally scans, the glorious Langtang Range towered in full sunlight against a deep blue sky. Our own whoops and laughter at the sight drowned out those haughty birds.

So we sat to rest, damp, cold, and enthralled with the beauty. The thin clouds overhead made the scene more appealing, offering Peter constantly shifting light and shadow for his camera. Refreshed, we plunged happily through a snowy forest to a campsite, tea and biscuits, and a leisurely gaze at a pink and orange sunset.

The next day we were climbing again. The sunlit mountains ahead offered incentive, despite the increasingly

Kali Gandaki River at Mustang Province.

thin, cold air.

For many trekkers, the third day is physically the most difficult: the legs are stretched but not yet seasoned, merely sore. But mentally, it's easier. The morning rituals of organizing for the contingencies of bright sun, rain, thirst, blisters, cold and possible high altitude headaches were ordinary, manageable, and welcome.

We had all slipped into the trekkers' mentality, and worries from our civilized lives were no longer baggage. Our thoughts and senses were alert and attuned to the quiet observance of ice patterns on puddles, the textures of rocks and mosses, and, with some trepidation, the changing density of the clouds overhead.

The day was warm and sunny. I walked on, occasionally talking about maps and routes and other wonderful places to go. More often I prefer to walk in silence. Sometimes I need to remind myself that, despite the ache in my left knee and a backpack that seems full of rocks, I am indeed thankful to be in this very place at this very moment. All it takes is a few quiet minutes, sitting, with a bottle of water and the pounding of my heart for company.

By lunchtime I was thoroughly exhausted from the physical exertion at high altitude. I decided I had had enough for one day. Our hot lunch of soup and carbohydrate variation #5 refueled Jim, Adam, and Peter, however, and they quickly set out for the final climb to Panch Pokhari, another 4,000 feet above us. David decided to stay behind with me, and we would make the final climb in the early morning.

As our three intrepid companions disappeared into more freezing snow and mist, our anxiety for them was overwhelmed by reality—we quickly fell asleep.

The next morning was bright and clear, so David and I started up, carrying the minimum for a day hike to Panch Pokhari. We passed the *mani* wall at the entrance to the pilgrimage path, and we wound, stumbled, and threaded our way across the icy ledges toward a passage between two jagged peaks. "How did they manage this treacherous trail in so much snow and ice?" "Why are we trying it now?"

Four hours later, we arrived in a snow-filled bowl and found our friends peacefully sitting beside a lake. The quiet was absolute except for a waterfall that sent a stream crashing thousands of feet into a small, emerald valley. A temple on the lip of the falls attested to the holiness of the site. Above and beyond, silhouetted against the sky, the northern rim of Nepal and Tibet hovered, clear and mysterious.

Peter had spent an uncomfortable night with Cheyne-Stokes Breathing, a common, though not terribly serious, symptom of oxygen deprivation. Certain of injury or worse if he attempted to descend in the dark, he stayed awake most of the night to keep himself breathing. When Doctor David delivered a short lecture on altitude sickness, Peter protested that he actually was suffering from *latitude* sickness, so far south of the Yukon.

That afternoon, the clouds and snow returned as we retraced the way to our camp. The sense of satisfaction at reaching the lakes was gradually replaced by the real business of trekking, putting one foot in front of the other.

By morning, our tents were covered with a solid layer of ice, but the chill in the air and the mountain silence enhanced the comfort and pleasure of our mugs of tea. As the sunlight crept down the snowy peaks to flood our

Above Naudanda: Perhaps this is why you came?

tents with warmth, a wave of tranquility and contentment passed through us all.

For an entire day we hiked down, with the air getting thicker and our bodies getting warmer. We peeled off layers of clothing as we approached terraced fields of millet above the stone-roofed villages. After endless upwards steps, the downward tracks made our knees trembled, and different muscles ached and cramped. As always, Pasang came bounding along, laughing, singing, and shouting to the animated porters on their way home.

We spent our last few days slowly hiking through a lovely valley of Tamang villages. We met many Nepalis, curious about the *sahibs* but pleasant and stand-offish enough to not become annoying. The weather stayed sunny and warm. And our moaning about the pain, chill, and damp of the first few days were, if not forgotten, at least replaced by the noise of the rushing rivers we followed. Our heads were still in the high mountains as our feet took us closer to our workday routines.

On any trek, the Nepali support team is as awe-inspiring as the scenery. Their strength is endless and their good humor is always contagious. When we fall into camp tired, hungry, and wondering why we are doing this, the crew is still hard at work making us comfortable. Setting up tents, gathering wood, hauling water, cleaning and cooking—they find the pleasures in every situation. When we fall asleep, feeling safe and satisfied with our day's efforts, their voices rise around the fire in the warmth and laughter of human contact.

Their satisfaction seems to be not in the achievement, but in the doing, together. Perhaps this, too, is why we went out trekking after all.

Appendix III:
Further Reading

We've suggested most of the books below based on their general interest, readability, and availability in bookstores and libraries. The list is in no way complete or particularly scholarly. It's intended only as a starting point for the curious traveler to Nepal.

Some of these books are more readily available in Nepal, so we've included the names and addresses of a few booksellers there. Major hotels sell some popular titles. Trekkers generally prefer not to carry a library with them, so there are lots of used books and "hole-in-the-wall" bookshops all over Kathmandu which buy, sell, and trade. They are good places to browse and find all sorts of bargain Asian editions, as well as foreign language books.

Bookstores

Educational Enterprises Ltd., Mahankalstan, Kathmandu (phone 223-749). Located on Kanti Path, diagonally across from the RNAC office at the top (arch-end) of New Road, under the temple. Carries a moderate selection, including fiction and children's books.

Ratna Pustak Bhandar, Bhotahity, Kathmandu (phone 221-88). Located on the left side of the small street that connects Kanti Path to Asantole, south of Bir Hospital. Carries a large and broad selection.

Pilgrims Book House, Thamel, Kathmandu (no phone). Located up the street from Kathmandu Guest House. Of the three stores, this one is best for leisurely browsing. Mostly Nepaliana and related topics. Lots of coffee-table books.

General Guidebooks

Apa Productions. *Insight Guide: Nepal*. Prentice Hall, 1986. The best general guidebook. Loaded with travel information. Buy it and take it with you.

Armington, Stan. *Trekking in the Nepal Himalaya*. Lonely Planet Publications, 1985. General guidebook with emphasis on specific trek routes and budget travel.

Bernstein, Jeremy. *The Wildest Dreams of Kew: A Profile of Nepal*. Simon & Schuster, 1970. An interesting travelogue.

Bezruchka, Stephen. *A Guide to Trekking in Nepal*. The Mountaineers, Seattle, WA, 1985. The best book available for exhaustive, detailed route information. Written primarily for the solo trekker.

Greenwald, Jeff. *Mister Raja's Neighborhood: Letters from Nepal*. John Daniel Publisher, Santa Barbara, CA, 1986. Delightful collection of anecdotes that capture the feel of the country.

Hagen, Toni. *Nepal, The Kingdom of the Himalayas*. Kummerley & Frey, Berne, Switzerland, 1980. An account by one of the first Western men to travel about Nepal. Beautiful pictures, good text.

Matthiessen, Peter. *The Snow Leopard*. Chatto & Windus, London, 1979. A spiritual journey.

Raj, Prakash A. *Kathmandu and the Kingdom of Nepal*. Lonely Planet Publications, 1985. A general, pocket-sized guide.

Reiffel, Robert. *Nepal Namaste*. Sahayogi Press, Kathmandu, 1980. Another good, general guide.

Suyin, Han. *The Mountain Is Young*. Jonathan Cape, London, 1958. A novel set in Pokhara in the 1950's.

History

Hopkirk, Peter. *Trespassers on the Roof of the World: The Race for Lhasa*. Oxford University Press, 1983. Fascinating accounts of early explorers. Captures the spirit of adventure and trekking.

Landon, Percival. *Nepal.* (Two volumes). Constable, London, 1928. Pre-printed by Bibliotheca Himalayica, New Delhi. Somewhat scholarly, but the best overall summary.

Peissel, Michel. *Tiger for Breakfast.* Hodder, London, 1966. Story of Boris Lissanevitch, the opening of Nepal to foreigners, and preparations for the King's coronation. Very readable and informative.

Regmi, Mahesh Chandra. A *Study of Nepali Economic History,* 1768-846. Manjusri, New Delhi, 1971. The development of the hill country economy.

Stein, R. A. *Tibetan Civilization.* Stanford University Press, 1972. Helpful in understanding the Buddhist groups in northern Nepal.

Art, Festivals, and Language

Anderson, Mary M. *Festivals of Nepal.* George Allen & Unwin, London, 1971. General and useful.

Aran, Lydia. *The Art of Nepal.* Sahayogi Press, Kathmandu, 1978. The art of Kathmandu Valley, from a religious perspective.

Karki, Tika B. and Shrestha, Chij K. *Basic Course in Spoken Nepali.* Kathmandu, 1979. The Peace Corps' language bible.

Kuly, Hullvard Kare. *Tibetan Rugs.* White Orchid Press, Bangkok, 1982. Beautiful pictures with a clear explanation of the tradition and symbolism.

Meerendonk, M. *Basic Gurkhali Dictionary.* Singapore, 1960. Its shirt-pocket size makes it very handy. Inexpensive but tends to self-destruct with frequent use, so buy two.

Religion, People, and Culture

Anderson, Walt. *Open Secrets: A Western Guide to Tibetan Buddhism.* Viking Penguin, 1980. A readable explanation from a Western perspective. Very useful in understanding Buddhism in Nepal.

Bista, Dor Bahadur. *People of Nepal*. Ratna Pustak Bhandar, Kathmandu, 1974. If you're interested in ethnic groups, this is the book you need.

Coburn, Broughton. *Nepali Aama: Portrait of a Nepalese Hill Woman*. Ross-Erikson, Santa Barbara, CA, 1982. Life in a Gurung village, told by an old woman, sensitively photographed by her friend.

Detmold, Gregory, and Rubel, Mary. *The Gods and Goddesses of Nepal*. Ratna Pustak Bhandar, Kathmandu, 1979. General, but useful.

Lal, Kesar. *Nepalese Customs and Manners*. Ratna Pustak Bhandar, Kathmandu, 1979. Contains useful information, though not in the style of Emily Post.

Valli, Eric. *The Honey Hunters of Nepal*. Abrams, New York, 1988. A fascinating look at a dying occupation.

Natural History

Fleming, R.L. Sr., R.L. Fleming Jr., and L.S. Bangdel. *Birds of Nepal*. Avalok, Kathmandu, 1979. The only book a serious birdwatcher would be seen with.

McDougal, Charles. *The Face of the Tiger*. Rivington Books, London, 1977. A study of the tigers of Chitwan National Park.

Mierow, Dorothy, and T. B. Shrestha. *Himalayan Flowers and Trees*. Sahayogi Press, Kathmandu, 1978. A useful field guide.

Mishra, Hemant Raj and Dorothy Mierow. *Wild Animals of Nepal*. Ratna Pustak Bhandar, Kathmandu, 1976. A survey with drawings.

Development

Haaland, Ane. *Bhaktapur: A Town Changing*. Bhaktapur Development Project, 1982. Describes goals and problems of the restoration of a living city. Wonderful "before" and "after" photographs.

Hillary, Edmund. *Schoolhouse in the Clouds*. Penguin Books, 1968. Sir Edmund's account of his early efforts on behalf of the Sherpas.

Mountaineering

Hackett, Peter. *Mountain Sickness: Prevention, Recognition, and Treatment.* American Alpine Club, New York, 1980. Written by the director of the Himalayan Rescue Association.

Rowell, Galen. *Many People Come, Looking, Looking.* The Mountaineers, Seattle, WA, 1980. Photographic record of trekking and climbing.

Wilkerson, James A. *Medicine for Mountaineering.* The Mountaineers, Seattle, WA, 1985. A practical guide for ordinary, non-medical folks.

There are numerous books recounting major Himalayan climbing expeditions. Look for titles by Chris Bonington, Maurice Herzog, Sir Edmund Hillary, John Hunt, and Reinhold Messner. We especially liked Arlene Blum's *Annapurna: A Woman's Place* (Granada Publishing, New York, 1980). Written for the non-climber, it contains all the elements of a mountaineering triumph, tragedy, and interesting social dynamics.

And don't forget *National Geographic Magazine's* frequent and excellent articles about Nepal.

About the Authors

Amy R. Kaplan first visited Nepal in 1968 and returned to live there from 1979 until 1986. During that time, she taught at the Lincoln School in Rabi Bhawan and spent much of her time developing and coordinating the school's trek program. She spent her holiday time trekking, as well. She now lives in Boulder, Colorado, where the mountains are a lot smaller but only a little less beautiful.

Michael Keller has lived in Nepal for the past five years while completing a graduate degree in Intercultural Communication. He operates a consulting service for researchers and scholars exploring areas of Nepali and Tibetan history and culture.

Jimmy Thapa, illustrator, is a freelance artist from Kathmandu. He is currently traveling the length of the Ganges, drawing temples, rituals, and pilgrims for a forthcoming book.

Stephen Trimble, photographer, writer, and naturalist, has recently published *Words from the Land: Encounters with Natural History Writing* and *Sagebrush Ocean: A Natural History of the Great Basin*. His photos have appeared in *Audubon*, *Newsweek*, and National Geographic books.

More Great Travel Books from Mustang Publishing

Europe for Free by Brian Butler. If you think a trip to Europe is just one long exercise in cashing traveler's checks, then this is the book for you! The author describes *thousands* of activities, sights, and fun things to see and do—and nothing costs one single lira, franc, or pfennig. "A *valuable resource*"—U.P.I. **$9.95**

Let's Blow thru Europe by Thomas Neenan & Greg Hancock. The essential guide for the "15-cities-in-14-days" traveler, *Let's Blow thru Europe* is hilarious, irreverent, and probably the most honest and practical guide to Europe ever written. Minor medieval cathedrals and boring museums? Blow 'em off! Instead, *Let's Blow* describes the key sites and how to see them as quickly as possible. Then, it takes you to the great bars, nightclubs, and restaurants that other guidebooks miss. Don't go to Europe without it! "*Absolutely hilarious!*"—*Booklist*. **$10.95**

Hawaii for Free by Frances Carter. How could anyone improve on Hawaii, America's paradise? Simple. Make a vacation there a whole lot cheaper! From free pineapple to free camping to a free brewery tour, this book describes hundreds of free things to do and see all over Hawaii—and nothing costs a penny. "*Invaluable*"—*Aloha Magazine*. **$6.95**

Australia: Where the Fun Is by Lauren Goodyear & Thalassa Skinner. The "land down under" has become tops in travel, and these recent Yale graduates spent a year exploring both the tourist sites and the little-known back alleys all over Austalia and New Zealand. From the best pubs in Sydney to the cheapest motel in Darwin to the most spectacular treks around Ayers Rock, this book details all the fun stuff—on and off the beaten path. *Available late* 1989. **$12.95**

————————

Mustang books should be available at your local bookstore. If not, order directly from us. Send a check or money order for the price of the book—plus $1.50 for postage *per book*—to Mustang Publishing, P. O. Box 9327, New Haven, CT 06533. Allow three weeks for delivery. *Foreign orders: U.S. funds only, please, and add $5.00 postage per book.*